Friendship
You and Your Dog

Friendship
You and Your Dog

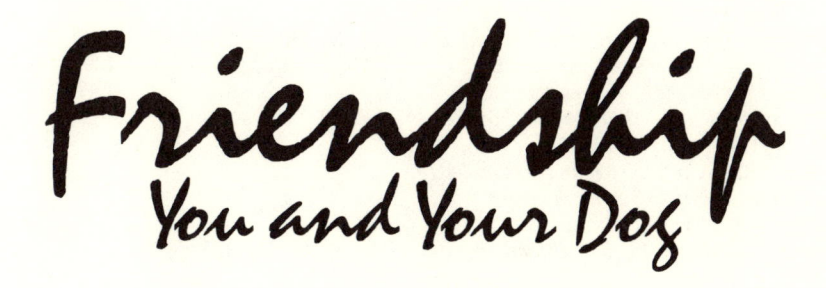

Judith M. Hancock

E. P. DUTTON NEW YORK

Grateful acknowledgment is made to the following for allowing the use of illustrations:

Canine Companions for Independence. pp. 162, 164
Rhonda L. Hodges Cline. pp. 3 (bottom), 13, 18, 19, 21, 23, 26, 42, 43, 45, 48, 49, 51, 57 (top), 60, 61, 75, 89, 95, 98, 101, 103, 108, 113, 115, 116, 119, 125, 138, 139, 140, 144, 145, 147, 187, 193, back of jacket
Mike Johnson. pp. 3 (top), 16, 50, 55, 174
Nancy P. Johnston. p. 169
Barbara Kemp. p. 175 (top and bottom left)
Hal Lauritzen. p. 175 (bottom right)
Marjorie Stewart. pp. 59, 63
Jean L. Turner. pp. 22, 57 (bottom), 99, 105, 111, 114, 117, 121, 123, 141

Copyright © 1986 by Judith M. Hancock
All rights reserved. Printed in the U.S.A.

No part of this publication may be reproduced or transmitted in any form or by any means, electronic or mechanical, including photocopy, recording, or any information storage and retrieval system now known or to be invented, without permission in writing from the publisher, except by a reviewer who wishes to quote brief passages in connection with a review written for inclusion in a magazine, newspaper, or broadcast.

Published in the United States by E. P. Dutton,
a division of New American Library,
2 Park Avenue, New York, N.Y. 10016.

Library of Congress Cataloging-in-Publication Data
Hancock, Judith M.
Friendship: you and your dog.

Bibliography: p.
Includes index.
1. Dogs. 2. Dogs—Training. 3. Dogs—Behavior.
I. Title.
SF426.H36   1986   636.7   86-6233

ISBN 0-525-24454-9

Published simultaneously in Canada
by Fitzhenry & Whiteside Ltd., Toronto

W

Designed by Steven N. Stathakis

10 9 8 7 6 5 4 3 2 1

First Edition

William
in Memory and Appreciation

Contents

Preface   xi

CHAPTER 1. CHOOSING YOUR DOG   1

    What Sort of Dog?   1
    Where to Find Your Dog   7
    Picking *the* Puppy   9

CHAPTER 2. DEVELOPMENT: WHAT TO EXPECT WHEN   11

    Neonatal Period   12
    Transitional Period   15
    Socialization Period   17
    Juvenile Period   25

CHAPTER 3. COMMUNICATION   28

    Communication Among Dogs   29
    Communication Among Humans   35

CONTENTS

CHAPTER 4. SOCIAL BEHAVIOR 44

    Some Examples of Social Behavior 44

CHAPTER 5. BUILDING THE BOND 53

    Togetherness 54
    Communicating with Your Dog 54

CHAPTER 6. LEARNING TO LEARN 66

    How the Dog Learns 67
    The Training Process 68
    Puppies Are Special 70

CHAPTER 7. COMPANIONSHIP TRAINING: HOME AND CAR 78

    Housetraining 79
    Car Etiquette 94

CHAPTER 8. COMPANIONSHIP TRAINING: BASIC OBEDIENCE 96

    Collar Training 97
    Lead Training 97
    Sit 104
    Come 106
    Stay 111
    Down 113
    Stand 117
    Back 118
    Fetch 119
    Jump 122
    Training the Older Dog 124
    Obedience Classes 125

CHAPTER 9. CARE AND FACILITIES   127

    Nutrition   127
    Exercise   134
    Facilities   138
    Weather Care   142
    Grooming   143
    Preventive Medicine   148

CHAPTER 10. FULFILLMENT   153

    Human Needs   153
    Urban Pressures   155
    The Living World   156
    The Dog   157
    Meeting Human Needs   159

CHAPTER 11. THE DOG'S HISTORY   166

    The Origin of the Dog   166
    Wolves   167
    Dog Breeding and Selection   172

A Final Word   179

APPENDIX 1. REPRODUCTION AND PRENATAL DEVELOPMENT   180

APPENDIX 2. PUPPY EVALUATION   185

APPENDIX 3. THE COMPANION DOG'S BASIC VOCABULARY   198

CONTENTS

Selected References   201

Acknowledgments   203

Index   205

Preface

Dogs and *people*: The words conjure up pictures as old as human civilization and as young as our own memories. The dogs of childhood in whom we could confide. When no one seemed to understand or to care, our dogs were there, knowing and caring. The dogs of country walks through rustling autumn leaves. The dogs who were our hunting companions. The dogs of shows. The dogs of uncertain heritage. The new little puppy bumbling along behind us. The old dog whose long life was all too brief a moment in ours. The dogs were ours and shared our lives, yet in another sense, they did not belong to us. We and they belonged to a common world, one whose roots trace back into the dim past of history. And beyond. Our mutual association speaks to us from the very core of our being. How did it all begin?

For me it began years ago when I was young and a little Sheltie came to share my life. He was the lone black pup in a kennel full of golden ones and I had eyes only for him. We lived together for all too few years, but during his life Jock hooked me forever in the world of dogs.

One day I went to a dog show, watched the obedience dogs perform, and resolved to train Jock to compete. My instructions

PREFACE

in this art were gleaned from the directions for a merit badge in dog training found in an old Boy Scout Handbook. My own education was just beginning. I bumbled through the basics while Jock, that bright and agreeable character, took it in good spirits and learned as best he could. With false confidence I entered a show. Watching the competition while waiting for our turn drained every ounce of confidence from me. Once in the ring, I was overwhelmed by my ignorance. Sensing that, unaccustomed to other dogs and lacking the security of knowledge, Jock behaved dreadfully. Our performance must yet rank among the most disastrous in the history of dog shows. But the day was saved by a man who cared enough to befriend a youngster and who, thus, made possible all the days that followed. As a trainer, he helped me solve our problems, and in a few weeks, under his guidance, Jock and I showed again with genuine confidence to win the Companion Dog title. The human friendship lasted a lifetime.

That was my start and all I needed to become more and more interested in dog training. Within a year, I had saved enough money to buy a second Sheltie, a female, of course, for training and breeding. Once they had been bred, the pregnancy was watched diligently, and with the greatest anticipation. I was told that puppies were usually born at night, but I knew they would arrive while I was in school. An impending birth was not considered sufficient reason to miss school, but neither could I go about the ordinary business of life with so momentous an event in the offing. A compromise, slightly dishonest, was reached. I endured days of classes before that prearranged message about an emergency at home at last brought my deliverance from math class to the unfolding drama in the corner of the kitchen. I had become a breeder.

In all my student years, I lived with my mind in the books and my heart with the dogs. Interest in dogs led me to a career as a biologist, first as a researcher, then as a teacher. Always, I was accompanied by a changing little band of Shelties of the same family, who rounded out my life. I lived with them and loved them. I did not know them.

It was Trice (pronounced "Treece"), Jock's great-great-great-great-great-granddaughter, who brought me to a real awareness of dogs. The litter of which she was a member was orphaned at one month of age, and I kept Trice and raised her with her grandfather. Just the two of them. She was a very peculiar character, unlike any dog I had ever had or known about. She fascinated me; I *had* to understand her. Thus began a study of dogs that gave me a far greater understanding and appreciation of them than I ever had.

In writing this book, I want to share some of my knowledge about dogs with you. I hope that it will enable you to understand your own dog better and to build a real friendship that brings pleasure to both of you.

You will learn about the physical and psychological needs of dogs and how best to provide for them. You will also learn about communications—both yours and your dog's. Basic training, building on communication, helps to build the bond between you and your dog into a truly deep relationship. Communicating effectively with your dog, the central theme of this book, is an unusual approach in books about dogs and their training. You will see, too, how dogs help fulfill some of our needs. Fulfilling mutual needs with a sensitive spirit is what this book is all about.

1

Choosing Your Dog

The choice of a companion to share one's life with is a very personal one. Ideally, the personalities of both human and dog should be taken into consideration to ensure mutual compatibility and realistic expectations. It really is a good idea, before obtaining a dog, to spend some time determining which type would be best for you and where to find it. There are some obvious factors to consider in selecting a prospective companion.

WHAT SORT OF DOG?

Purebred or Not? A purebred dog is a member of a breed recognized by the American Kennel Club (AKC) or other national registry system in this country or abroad. At present, the AKC recognizes 126 breeds. Nonpurebred dogs are of mixed ancestry.

The purebred's big advantage is its predictability. Physical and behavioral characteristics have been stamped into it by generations of selective breeding. Thus, purchasing a Boxer puppy guarantees that it will grow up to look like and act like a Boxer, not a Scottie or a Setter. Qualities that are of interest to prospective owners—size, coat, color, soundness, excitability, responsiveness—are predictable in the purebred, unknown for the mixed-breed, and somewhat predictable for the crossbreed (from a cross of two purebreds). An advantage usually attributed to the nonpurebred dog, but not limited to it, is stamina. That characteristic can be achieved in any breeding if the breeder is concerned about it.

Serious breeders breed purebreds. They are students of their breed, knowledgeable about it as well as about canine matters in general. They are fascinated by the challenges of selective breeding, enjoying the fellowship of other enthusiasts and the opportunities to compare dogs and the sport of competition. They do not deny that there are problems with purebreds. However, working with purebred animals is the only way in which the problems can be studied, their possible inheritance determined, and their frequency reduced through controlled breeding. This is not possible with nonpurebreds, whose heritage is uncertain.

Small or Large? Size varies enormously. The tiniest of the toy dogs are about eight inches tall at the top of the back; the tallest (the Irish Wolfhound) stands about three feet tall. Weight varies from about 3 to 170 pounds. Take the size of the mature dog into consideration in selecting a puppy, particularly in terms of space, food, and exercise (see Chapter 9). Large dogs, obviously, require more of all of these than do little ones. Generally, large dogs do best in the country, where they have more room. Although I have known city people with large dogs (and the dedication to match) who walked miles daily to keep their dogs in condition, most city dwellers, particularly those in apartments, would find a small dog a better choice.

Male or Female? There are advantages and disadvantages to each gender. The male is the more impressive in appearance, with a

A dog is a friend for life.

proud bearing; he is more outgoing and, in general, does not get along easily with other males. In the long-coated breeds, he has a heavier coat than the female. If he has been bred, he may have a desire to roam; he certainly will have a roving eye. The female comes in heat twice a year and requires particular attention during that time. Usually, she is content with her own territory and is less interested in expansion than is the male. Both make fine companions; the choice is a matter of personal preference.

Neither males nor females should be permitted to roam, whatever their interests might be. Although it is not necessary for their health or happiness to do so, their safety and the rights of other people require that they stay at home.

Many people object to neutering dogs on emotional grounds, feeling that the quality of a dog's life is adversely affected. This is not true; dogs do not need sexual activity and do not think about what might have been. Neutering simplifies your life and helps curtail the burgeoning pet population. Do consider it seriously.

Puppy or Adult? The formative and adaptable puppy, so easily able to respond to a new person and to accept a new life, is probably preferable. Many people consider that a half-grown or adult dog is easier to take on "because it is already housebroken." This may or may not be true in a new situation. Furthermore, an adult may, and probably does, have some other problems; inquire carefully before acquiring one. It is, however, unfair to assume that older dogs are utterly undesirable as companions. Whatever the age of the dog you acquire, you should expect to spend a good bit of time with your pet while adapting it to your way of life.

Shorthaired or Long? There are two types of coat: smooth- or shorthaired, and long-haired. Long hair is extremely variable. It may be short and dense (German Shepherd), long and dense (Collie), long and silky (Yorkshire Terrier), short and wiry (terriers), long and curly (Poodle), or long and corded (Komondor). Some long coats lie flat against the dog's body whereas others stand off from it. The latter are thick with a woolly undercoat.

Grooming long-haired dogs is more involved than it is for smooth-haired ones (see Chapter 10). The standards of many long-haired breeds require styling, or at least frequent brushings, to keep the dog comfortable and attractive. This factor should be taken into account when selecting a dog.

All dogs shed. It is simply a matter of the length and quantity of the hair shed, not whether it will occur. People who have dogs should expect fur in the house. If your housekeeping standards cannot take that, don't have a dog.

How About Appearance? Some dogs have an imposing carriage with an aura of nobility about them, and other dogs have a more ordinary appearance. Body build and coat, as well as carriage, contribute to appearance. Some dogs appear to be grotesque, but what is repugnant to some is attractive or interesting to others. It is a personal matter. In some breeds, the ears or tails are cut to produce the breed's characteristic appearance (Doberman Pinschers, for example). Some people are repelled by this practice; if you are one of them, choose another breed, because your dog should be attractive to you.

What Sort of Temperament? Temperament is the primary consideration. It is molded by experience, training, and handling, but only within the limits set by inheritance, and ranges from gentle to aggressive with complex and subtle shadings. Temperament is a breed characteristic, strongly influenced by heredity. It is neither reasonable nor fair to expect a dog to be other than what its inheritance dictates. A terrier puppy has a terrier's temperament and cannot be spaniellike. Accept the dog for what it is or choose another breed. Temperament must be something you can live with happily.

There is, of course, no guarantee that you will select the best temperament, but there are some factors you should look for. Talk with the previous owner, see where and how the dog lived, watch its interactions with other dogs (if possible) and with you. If you are choosing a puppy, see "Picking *the* Puppy," (p. 9). Should you prefer an older dog, take it home and let it live with you for several days, or weeks preferably, to see whether you are compatible.

One of the points that you should be aware of is that when puppies are raised without social interactions with people and other dogs during the formative periods (see Chapter 2), the personality is altered in ways that persist throughout the dog's life. The extent of the effect varies with the inherent temperamental makeup of the puppy and the duration of isolation. At the least, the personality is flat and underdeveloped or "quirky," although the animal is capable of functioning normally. Under the worst circumstances the dog is psychotic.

Personality, a quality of the individual, develops from both heredity and experience. In living with your dog, you are molding its personality in accordance with your own. This book will make you more aware of natural canine temperament and help you to mold your dog's personality into that of a good companion for you.

Health. Health is another important consideration. The health of a litter begins with the mother and starts from the time she is a mere infant. Conscientious breeders have dogs that are well fed, have received all the appropriate inoculations, and are glowing with good health. The dogs are eager and active, their eyes sparkling, their coats shiny, the stock basically healthy.

Soundness is an aspect of health. Physically sound animals are put together so that all parts function properly and the dog moves correctly. Unsound ones have structural errors that make them tire more easily and that may create medical problems as they age. Mentally sound dogs act in typical canine fashion; extreme and unpredictable behavior is unsound.

WHERE TO FIND YOUR DOG

Breeders. If you are interested in a purebred dog, the best source is the serious hobby or professional breeder. This person may not have a kennel, in the sense of runs and buildings, but he or she does have a kennel name, the trademark used to register the dogs. The facilities are clean, and the breeder is liked by the dogs. Look for a knowledgeable and enthusiastic approach as the breeder honestly and openly discusses the dogs, the line they come from and their strengths and weaknesses as representatives of the breed. Notice how the breeder raises the dogs and what has been done with them in training and showing. The breeder should have dreams and plans, not merely a bunch of pups. He will think his breed is the greatest of all. No doubt, he will be interested in you and will ask some leading questions because he wants something more than money: he wants a quality home with the right sort of people for his puppy. He is literally selling happiness. He wants to be sure that the little creature in whom he has already invested so much will be well treated.

Breeders with limited space often raise promising pups for show or breeding and sell those that did not turn out as hoped to good homes, often at a reduction in price. The deficiencies may be purely cosmetic and have no effect on the ability of the dog to be a good companion, but as unsoundness is often one of the reasons for selling, you must be careful. Ideally, the dog should go to someone who knows it and who is willing to take the time and has the patience and understanding to make the transition as easy as possible. Truly happy relationships do result. Often this is the best route for an older person.

It is a good idea to know what is meant by *pet quality* and the price it entails in the particular breed and locale. The term refers to a puppy that is of neither show nor breeding quality; the dog may be too large or small or have undesirable markings, but more often the term indicates unsoundness. A pet-quality puppy usually costs several hundred dollars. Certainly, it should not have faults that will affect the quality of its life.

Beware of those breeders who say that their puppies are show dogs but are vague about details, seem evasive, rush you into making a choice, or appear more concerned with money than homes.

The breeder should be someone who is willing to answer your questions, one in whom you can have confidence and a feeling of rapport. Talk to several breeders to make comparisons.

A good place to find breeders, as well as to see the variety of purebred dogs available, is a dog show. Breeders also advertise in newspapers and dog magazines.

Casual Litters. A friend or an advertiser with a litter of pups, although not so knowledgeable as the serious breeder, may nonetheless have followed good advice in raising the litter and may well have healthy and happy animals. Often the puppies are somewhat less expensive, but they may have had plenty of attention and can make fine companions.

Pounds or Shelters. Dogs in municipal pounds or humane society shelters are strays or abandoned, discarded, and no longer wanted pets. They are housed and fed. How well they are treated and how much attention they receive depend on the concern of those who care for them. The attempt is to place desirable animals in homes at a minimal cost, usually the license fee, rabies shots if required by law, and frequently, the charge for neutering. But many a good match is made, and the person feels particularly good about saving a dog from death and giving it a good home.

Pet Stores. The pet store is not the place to get your dog. Pet-store puppies have been mass-produced at some distant location and shipped to arrive at their cutest age. Usually that means that they left their first home too soon. It is not possible to know how the pups were raised previous to shipping, but it is unlikely that they received much individual handling. They certainly do not receive it in the store. They are clean, well fed, and displayed to be appealing to the buying public, but they lack attention, affection, and the opportunity to learn by exploring and playing in a normal environment. These puppies are considered merchandise. The needs of a sensitive, living creature cannot be met by treating it in the same way as television sets, groceries, or clothing. Pet-store pups are only a fraction of what they might have become. A pity.

PICKING *THE* PUPPY

Choosing *the* puppy out of a whole litter of appealing puppies is difficult, and usually very subjective.

Often the puppy is chosen for its pretty markings, cuteness, or sex. Problems can develop that might have been avoided if the person had been more objective in choosing. Again, as opposed to those less knowledgeable, the serious breeder is better able to inform you and help you make your best choice.

At first, watch the litter together, eating, sleeping, playing. Some pups take the lead in activities, and others tend to hold back. Because they will not live together and because puppies behave differently in a group than they do alone, each puppy should also be observed individually. Tests have been devised that can aid in making an evaluation of the puppies (see Appendix 2).

What is the best age for a puppy to leave the litter? Never under seven weeks. The seventh week is a good time. The pup has been part of the litter long enough to have developed canine relationships and not so long that it is cast into a behavioral mold (see Chapter 2). The eight- to ten-week period, a sensitive age, may not be the best time. It is fine if the puppy is well adjusted and going to a home similar to its breeder's, but shipping or moving from the country to the city may be too hard on the puppy. Wait until after the tenth week for changes like these, that are stressful for the pup.

Little puppies adjust to new situations, but older ones take longer to do so. The longer a puppy remains with a person, the more the bond between them grows. Forming new bonds takes a while. The ease with which a pup, of any age, can take on a new situation depends on its flexibility and the understanding of its new human.

2

Development: What to Expect When

As the owner of a new puppy, you need to be aware of the changing capabilities of this little creature as it grows.

Birth, a major event in development, is marked by an abrupt change of environment. A new life is suddenly thrust into a world of sound and light (neither of which a puppy can perceive), where it must breathe and eat. It is the first stress of life, and, not surprisingly, some cannot survive it.

Those who have studied development have found that puppyhood can be divided into several periods with characteristic events taking place in each. The investigators are not in complete agreement about the number of periods or the duration of each. This is to be expected because development is a continuous process, and the descriptive periods, employed for convenience in studying the process, are somewhat arbitrary. Individual puppies may deviate from them and still be completely normal. The periods of puppyhood described here are the most commonly used ones: neonatal, transitional, socialization, and juvenile.

NEONATAL PERIOD
0–14 DAYS

The first period begins at birth and ends when the eyes and ears open at about the fourteenth day. During this time, the pup becomes established as a breathing and feeding animal in the world outside of its mother. It is still completely dependent on her, though.

The newborn puppy has a sausagelike body with a large round head stuck on one end, stubby legs, and a tail hung off the other end. The hair is short and plush. The tiny ear flaps are flattened back against the skull with the canals grown shut and the puppy unable to hear. The eyes are closed. The little creature slides out of its mother in its watery sac and is immediately cleaned and dried. It looks as ineffectual and fetal as it is.

Major changes begin immediately. As the mother works her pups over, they gasp and pull air into their lungs for the first time. Her massaging tongue encourages rhythmic breathing contractions. Circulatory changes take place rather quickly, with the loss of the umbilical circulation and the acquisition of the heart-lung circuit. The digestive system is geared to the digestion of milk and begins to work as soon as milk arrives in the stomach.

The nervous system changes most during the neonatal period. The brain is incompletely developed at birth and, consequently, so are the puppy's capabilities. It has a few instinctive behaviors. One of these is the *rooting reflex*. The head moves randomly sideways, and when it contacts a soft, warm object (like the mother's belly), it moves up and down. That action ruffles the fur and locates a nipple. The senses of smell and taste are developed sufficiently to help the puppy locate the milk. The *suckling reflex* is another instinct. The puppy's mouth opens, and its overly large tongue wraps around the nipple. Pulling to obtain milk is done with the cheek, neck, and shoulder muscles. The forepaws push against the breast in a

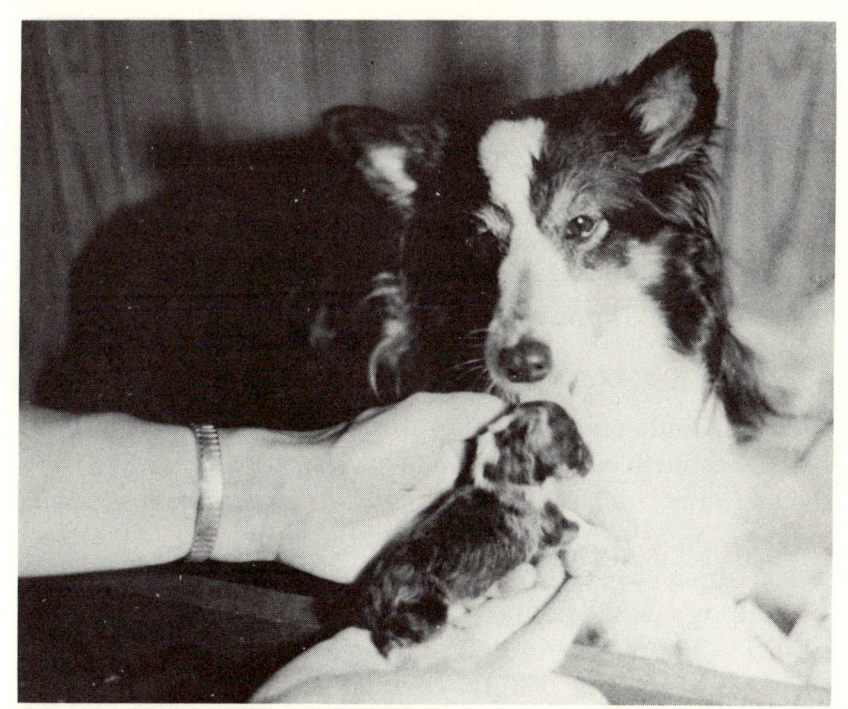

This baby Shetland Sheepdog, weighing four ounces, is just a few minutes old. Her mother's soft and gentle expression as she licks her puppy dry is characteristic of good maternal behavior.

rhythmic, kneading motion further to assist milk release. Another instinct is the ability to distinguish temperatures. A puppy moves toward warmth and away from hot and cold.

Neonatal movement is a *crawl*. The belly rests on the floor and is pulled forward by the forelegs. As development proceeds, the muscles of the legs become stronger, and the puppy is able to use them more effectively. The hindlegs brace and scramble while nursing, and the forelegs knead vigorously. The puppies do not get far away from the mother at this time. If they are separated, the body moves around in a circle with the random head movements until the mother is relocated. Some mothers assist by nuzzling or picking up the pups.

In addition to the senses of smell and taste, the neonatal puppy also has touch, balance, pain, and temperature senses. Most of these are vague, owing to the condition of the nervous system. Although the puppy can feel its mother's tongue or a human hand, these have no meaning and it is unable to locate the feeling. The mother's attentions act to bond her to her offspring; they are not able to relate to her. By the same token, neither can they relate to petting, although it is a good idea to begin such attentions at birth so that as perceptions develop, the stimulation is present to give an immediate and pleasurable association.

Brain and spinal cord are sufficiently developed at birth to permit instinctive and reflexive behaviors to occur. The parts of the brain that are best developed are those that are most necessary: the areas regulating heartbeat, breathing rate, and digestion. Temperature control has not developed. The only way that the puppy's body temperature can be maintained is by its behavior. Puppies lie on top of one another and cuddle up to their mother. Under natural conditions, they live in a small, low-roofed den, which helps hold in body warmth and maintain their temperatures high enough to allow metabolism to proceed normally. The brain centers that regulate wakefulness also have not developed. Puppies spend most of the time in an activated sleep, with the body muscles twitching and quivering frequently.

Most poorly developed of all of the parts of the nervous system is the *cerebrum*, the part of the brain concerned with the interpretation of information from the senses, directing voluntary movements, learning, and memory. There are relatively few cells in the cerebrum at birth, but the numbers increase during the neonatal period. These cells have long, branching projections that connect with other such cells, making an enormously complex network for the transmission of information within the cerebrum and extending from it to other parts of the brain and the rest of the body. This information is transmitted electrically. Electrical activity in the neonatal puppy's brain is very weak. Although there are differences in responsiveness and coordination in different parts of the body, in general, responses are slow and coordination poor. For example, puppies are unable to excrete without the external stimulation provided by the mother's licking the anal and genital areas. Nerve connections simply have not formed by this age. By virtue of her constant attention, elimination does take place, and the puppies and den are kept clean.

Neonatal puppies can make a plaintive cry when they are separated, cold, or hungry. Even though they cannot hear themselves, the mother can and anxiously comes to the rescue when she hears their cries, supplying warmth, food, and contact to relieve their distress.

The neonatal pup is little more than a fetus in another world. It is hardly in communication with that world, however. It knows nothing. It is not aware. It responds only to those things that actually touch it, and then it is unaware of where it was touched. It is a being isolated from its world.

TRANSITIONAL PERIOD
14–20 DAYS

Transition is a brief period during which the completely helpless neonatal animal changes into a baby dog. The period begins with the opening of the eyes and ears on about the fourteenth day and ends when the puppy begins to respond to sounds at about the twentieth day.

The time at which the eyes and ears open is quite variable, with both the breed and individually, and occurs between the tenth and fourteenth day after birth. Development is not complete at this time, however. When the eyes first open, they respond to light, but the puppy is unable to see. Vision gradually develops, as eye and brain development are completed. Puppies do not act as if they can hear until they startle at sounds about six days after the ear canals are open. Startling or moving away from a sound is indicative that the puppy can

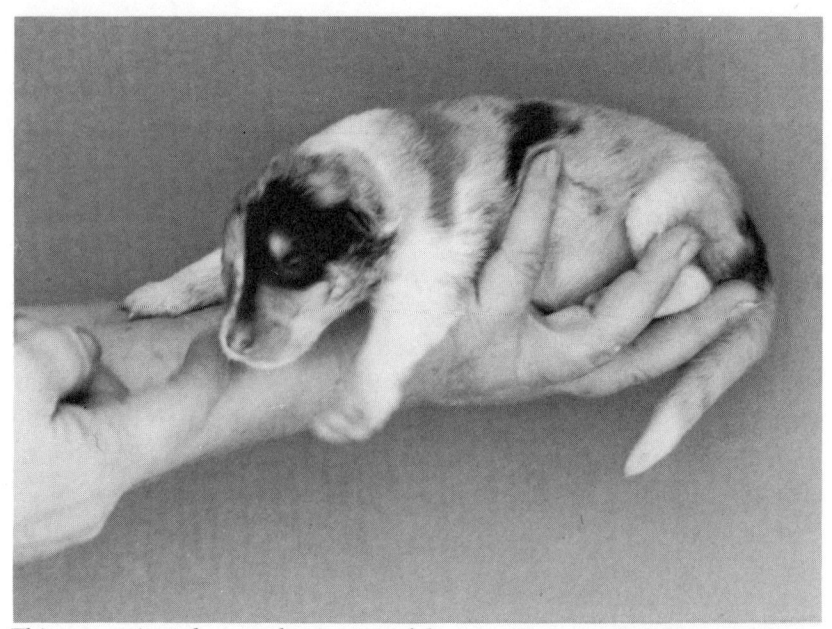

This puppy is at the very beginning of the transitional period. The eyes have barely opened and are quite sensitive to light. In appearance, the puppy has changed little since birth.

hear. By three weeks, all of the senses are functional, at least to some extent, as shown by the puppy's behavior.

As soon as the eyes open, the puppy begins to crawl backward as well as forward. As the nerves and muscles develop, the pup is able to get its feet under its body and to stand unsteadily. Most puppies walk by three weeks.

The neonatal puppy has a single means of eating: by suckling. By the time of the transitional phase, the puppy can also lap. Teeth are visible in the gums and first break through on about the twentieth day. Puppies cannot chew food until they have teeth, but they begin to make chewing motions earlier.

The nervous system has advanced considerably since birth. The number of cells, their extensions and branches, has increased greatly, and interconnections have been established between the cerebrum and other parts of the brain and the body. These connections make it possible for the puppy to stand and to walk, as well as being able to urinate and defecate without external stimulation. Puppies stagger away from the nest to excrete as soon as they are able, although the mother still cleans up after them. The cerebrum has enlarged; electrical activity has increased. Body temperature control is established; the pups sleep apart from one another instead of piling up, indicating that they are able to maintain their own body warmth. Activated sleep gradually diminishes as the brain's sleep center develops, so that by three weeks, the body relaxes in sleep, as the adult's does.

Because the nervous system has developed further, the puppy is able to do more than it could during the neonatal period. Typical canine behavior begins at the end of the transitional period when the pups begin to notice others—littermates, mother, humans—and to interact with them. They wag their tails and begin to paw at each other. They lick a human face. They still use their distress cry if separated. They also begin to learn. At first, learning is only a simply conditioned response. The puppy withdraws from, then learns to avoid unpleasant situations such as the scratchy, the cold, the sharp, the smelly. It is attracted to pleasant and comfortable situations, which it then learns to seek out. It merely discriminates pleasant from unpleasant without further associations at this time. As these behavioral changes take place, the heart rate begins to fluctuate with pleasant and unpleasant associations, the beginnings of emotional responses.

Thus, in the period of about a week, a very different sort of little creature—a dog—begins to emerge. It eats and moves as a dog does, if clumsily. It has all of its senses and is extremely sensitive to its world. It has begun to learn and to interact with others.

SOCIALIZATION PERIOD
3–12 WEEKS

The puppy's childhood begins at about three weeks and lasts until sexual maturity. It is divided into two periods: socialization and juvenile. The *socialization* period, from three to twelve weeks, is a special period of its own, marked by the development of social interactions and attachments. It is *the* period for behavior development.

Physical development taking place in this period alters the puppy's mode of life. The baby teeth break through the gums during the fourth week (twenty-one to twenty-eight days), and the puppy begins to chew. The eye and the visual-control centers in the cerebrum are completely developed by the eighth week. Brain development is also complete by that time, as indicated by the presence of adult-type brain waves. The puppy grows rapidly. It can run as well as walk, although awkwardly. It is unable to sustain activity for long and still sleeps a great deal.

At the beginning of the socialization period, the 21-day-old puppy looks like a little dog. He can hear and see, but his navy-blue eyes don't focus very well. He has just finished eating, and flecks of yogurt dot his face.

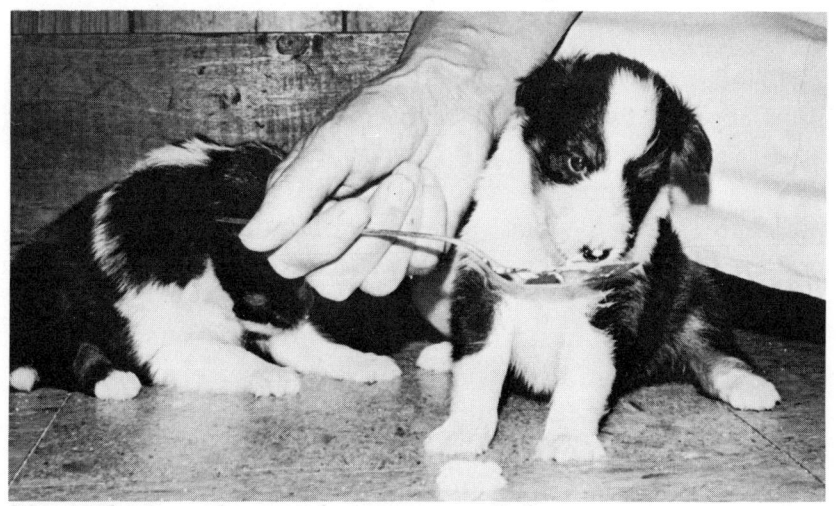

Weaning begins with yogurt from a spoon at 21 days.

The major changes, though, are behavioral ones. Weaning, which takes place during this period, marks the onset of several changes in behavior. The eruption of teeth indicates that the digestive tract has developed so that it can digest solid food. In wolves and dogs living on their own, the mother begins to leave her ravenous offspring to hunt. At first, she provides them with vomited food; as they get older, she carries back freshly killed prey. The habit of carrying fresh catches back to the den continues until the puppies have their permanent teeth and are able to hunt for themselves at four to five months of age. Nursing gradually tapers off.

When puppies are raised by humans, the weaning process is managed differently and with variable degrees of success as far as subsequent development is concerned. One method is *abrupt weaning:* the puppies nurse for a predetermined time, three or four weeks, and then are fed a prepared diet and have no further contact with their mother. An alternative method is *gradual weaning:* the puppies' diet is supplemented by feedings, and the mother continues to nurse them. She is with her pups on an intermittent basis, and particularly at night. They know the comfort and security of the familiar; she licks them, and they cuddle to her and nurse.

Under natural conditions, the mother begins to wean her pups at about five weeks. She discourages them from nursing by growling and snapping at them when they come up to her. The startled puppies back off. They learn to distinguish her moods by her behavioral signals, to recognize when they may and may not nurse. The weaning process is the first rejection of their lives.

The mother's tactics may seem overly rigorous, and one might expect them to affect the puppies adversely. This is not the case, however. The puppies readily associate their actions with the mother's refusal. They learn to accept the discipline that is promptly and unequivocally administered. They can understand. In abrupt weaning, the mother's interactions with her pups suddenly stops and emotional effects may result.

The puppies pester their mother and any other adults and are promptly disciplined. As this happens, the pups cling together in a litter pack. They do things together: eating, sleeping, excreting, playing. Their play is rough, perhaps in imitation of the adult behavior toward them. They also learn to use a common area, away from their nest, as a toilet. This natural habit can readily be used in housetraining (see Chapter 7).

On their own, puppies of this age do not venture away from the nest and toilet areas. They remain close to each other and to familiar surroundings, thus becoming attached to both. They are wary of the new. But their sense of curiosity also develops and they begin to investigate. New objects are approached cautiously with the head and neck extended and the legs braced. The pups are prepared to flee if need be and gradually move in closer if everything seems all right. Their tails wag in friendly overtures toward other living creatures.

The puppies have learned about rejection and about fear. Both are normal parts of life. The puppy's typical reaction when its mother rebuffs nursing attempts is one of surprise and retreat, followed by new attempts until the lesson has been learned. The reaction to fear is immobility. Puppies crouch or

The puppy fear reaction. With his lowered head and body position, dejected expression, and forepaw lifted tentatively, this puppy seems to shrink with fear.

In a strange place, the puppies, 54 days old, follow their person closely.

flatten themselves and huddle together. They seem smaller and less conspicuous. The puppy fear reaction begins with weaning and lasts until about the fourteenth week. The period between eight and ten weeks is particularly sensitive. This is a fear imprint stage, and memories of something frightening tend to remain with the dog for life. Obviously, it is desirable to avoid frightening situations then.

The most frightening situation for puppies is being alone in a strange place. When old enough to be taken to new places,

This puppy is the same as the one shown on page 18. Here he is in the middle of the socialization period (62 days old), or about at the age when puppies go to their new homes. All of his faculties are well developed, his head has elongated, the white face blaze has narrowed somewhat, and he responds well to people and other dogs.

The puppies, 63 days old, have gone visiting for the first time. The crate door has just been opened. This puppy is alert, interested, and cautious. After a few minutes, he stepped out of the crate and began to explore the new surroundings. Little sister followed his lead, and shortly they felt at home and were playing happily.

the pups stay in a tight little pack and follow closely behind mother or a person. If a pup does become isolated, it panics; it may freeze, or it may run away, and it cries piteously to attract attention. In the wild, isolation is dangerous because the pups are then vulnerable to attack by predators. The same fear reactions can occur when a puppy is taken from the litter. Alone and afraid, it can be expected to show fear or even to panic.

Serious breeders are aware of the crucial nature of the socialization period in forming the puppy's temperament and responses. Some breeders set up a structured learning situation to ensure that their puppies have been exposed to a variety of new experiences during this period. Others are more casual, but arrive at the same end point. That is, the puppies have had opportunities to meet new scents, sights, sounds, surfaces, and people so that they are poised and can move into a new home comfortably.

A litter raised in the house does not need a structured adjustment program. The puppies have been exposed to the whole gamut of normal household activities from the first moment of their awareness. They have been handled by different people, male and female, children and adults, and have no problem adjusting to new homes.

Structured "socializing" can easily be overdone. The puppy first needs to find its place in the group to which it was born: litter, other dogs, people, other animals. It needs to become acquainted with the physical environment. Once these associations have been established, the puppy should gradually expand its world so that it can learn and be able to meet new situations comfortably. If this is not done during the socialization period, the puppy usually grows up to be overly fearful of anything new, akin to a wild animal. As important as new experiences are, so are quiet and familiar settings. Puppies can be overstimulated, receiving a barrage of experiences too fast to allow them to cope. Their reactions, then, are like those of small children with too much Christmas morning excitement. After some excitement and new experiences, the puppies should be put into their pen in a quiet spot to rest or to play by themselves. Puppies also need some private time with their people without the rest of the litter. This activity encourages individuality and makes the transition to the typical only-dog status easier for the puppy.

Socialization involves far more than meeting new experiences. It essentially involves the establishment of the natural hierarchy within the litter and the relationship of the puppies to adults (see Chapter 3). The litter's organization of leader and followers is determined by its own interactions by the seventh week. Puppies show deference to adult dogs, but the real leader of the social order is man. During this period, the puppies learn to accept the person who takes care of them as their leader and to establish the relationship of other members of the household to this individual. All of these relationships should be permitted to take place naturally. The puppies, then, have learned early in life that theirs is a nondemanding and accepting role within a larger group.

Abrupt weaning tends to interfere with this natural socialization. If puppies are sold before the litter leadership role is determined, they do not easily associate with other dogs. They may become withdrawn, indifferent, or overly aggressive, depending on their inherent temperament. On the other hand, if a litter is kept together with insufficient human contact through the fourteenth week, the puppies are unable to socialize properly with humans. Abrupt weaning, insufficient contact, and early sales, all of which are attributes of the mass production of dogs, create subsequent behavior problems. It is remarkably easy to avoid these problems by natural puppy rearing.

The puppy at this age is a winsome, appealing, affectionate little creature. It learns readily from its senses, from its curiosity, and from its interactions with others, especially its mother and its human leader. It is vulnerable and impressionable. Although it is important that the impressions be good ones, no environment is perfect. It is, therefore, more important that the puppy be raised to have a flexible personality that will enable it to roll easily with life's punches. The attitude of the person who raises the puppy is critical. It should be casual, as open and friendly as a puppy's. Neither oversolicitousness nor a lack of caring is a healthy attitude for puppy-raisers.

JUVENILE PERIOD
12 WEEKS–SEXUAL MATURITY

The final period of puppyhood begins at twelve weeks and lasts until sexual maturity. Twelve weeks marks the time at which the puppy first begins to explore away from the nest-and-toilet area on its own. While it does so, it is not secure and stays close to its leader. It still can be easily frightened but gradually acquires more confidence with more experience.

Several changes begin at about four months. The permanent teeth come in accompanied by a great deal of chewing. This phase is over by about six months. In long-headed breeds, the elongation begins at three to four months. The growth rate begins to slow down after the fourth month, and the body begins to fill out. Proportions change. As the muscles develop, the pup becomes stronger and better coordinated; the maturing process may take two years or more to complete. The coat, in long-haired breeds, begins to grow during the fourth month, so that by five months, the puppy really looks like its relatives.

The four-to-five-month-old pup is at a difficult stage. It has learned a lot; it is able to do many things; it is venturesome. Often, it is also cocky, assertive, and bratty. This is the time when the pup establishes itself as an individual and pushes against authority, both human and canine. Yet, at the same time, it is an emotional, fearful, and dependent creature. Se-

The five-month-old juvenile looks like an adult, except for the length of coat, but she is still very immature.

curity is achieved by discipline, which sets the bounds of acceptable conduct. The pup needs training but is easily distracted and quite excitable. As the attention span is short, training sessions must be brief.

After this rebellious adolescent stage, the puppy gradually begins to settle down into more mature types of behavior.

The onset of sexual maturity varies both with the breed and with the individual. It is determined by the capacity to reproduce and is recognized by the first heat in the female and active sperm in the male. Behavioral signs indicate maturity. Males lift their legs to urinate and usually show at least some aggressiveness toward other males. Courting and mating behavior is apparent in both sexes. Maturity depends on the rate of development, a breed characteristic, and varies from about six to eighteen months.

3

Communication

Although there are other trainers who also use gentle methods, or *inducive training*, my approach, emphasizing natural communication, is unusual. Communication is the key to all teaching, canine or human, but with the dog you must break the language barrier and reach it in ways it can understand. You cannot teach a dog by explanation as you can another person, but neither must you train by physical force. You must communicate your desires in words and by showing the dog what you want. Once you realize how much dogs communicate with each other by nonverbal signals and how aware they are of subtle nuances of your body and facial expression and variations in tone of voice, you will see the importance of communication in dog training. You will find that this book devotes considerable attention to the human side of the relationship. Other trainers and books pay scant attention to the owner, and none of them discusses human communication. Yet the whole quality of the training a dog receives is dependent on its human's knowledge, expectations, attitude, and emotional control. To the perceptive person, training a dog turns out to be, rather surprisingly, a way to learn about oneself.

At first glance, there are so many differences between canine and human communication that it would seem that we could hardly communicate at all. Obviously, that is not true; you will see that there are many similarities.

COMMUNICATION AMONG DOGS

In order to communicate effectively with the dog, you need to understand its natural communications system. All the *canids* (wild and domestic members of the dog family) have inherited reflexes present at birth that are the basis for *instincts*, hereditary behavioral patterns characteristic of the particular canid. As the brain develops and as more information is stored in it, different kinds of responses begin to take place. Learning from experiences augments the simpler instincts and expands the animal's capabilities.

Our knowledge of canine communication comes from wolves as well as dogs, and hence you will find wolves mentioned in several places in this book, and particularly in Chapter 11.

Vocal Communication. All canids have extremely good hearing and consequently use sounds in a wide range of tonal variations to communicate with one another.

The earliest puppy sound is a mewing cry. It is a distress call that occurs in the first days after birth and indicates that the pup is hungry, too hot or cold, or in pain. The sound is seldom heard with puppies that are well fed and comfortable; therefore, it indicates that something is wrong. The mother becomes frantic when she hears the cry. After a time, the mew changes to a whine, but its message remains the same: the puppy wants something. The whine is retained into adulthood, with assorted variations in tone and intensity, and is used as an enticement, in greeting, or as a sign of submission. Puppies also squeal when play gets rough. Whining or squealing may be used as an appeasement when the puppy is disciplined as well.

Barking is the major communications sound of the dog. In maturity, it is a sharp staccato, repeated frequently with varieties of tone and meaning. The puppy's shrill bark is first heard, often to its own amazement, at about three weeks of age. Some of the adult barks are the greeting, the warning, the aggressive, the frustrated, the fussy. The *greeting* bark, high-pitched with an eager, excited tone, greets family members on their return, or on other special occasions, like the advent of a new day. The *warning* bark is deeper and alerts the group. The *aggressive* bark is deeper still and signifies a threat. The *frustrated* bark is high-pitched, frantic, and continued for a long time. The *fussy* bark is also high-pitched and prolonged, with a scolding tone. A bark variant is the *woof,* in which the mouth is closed and the sound subdued. Wolves bark less frequently than dogs. A bark or two may be given as a challenge or as an alert to the pack; woofing does the same more quietly.

The *growl* communicates threat or aggression. In encounters, only the more senior dog or leader wolf growls; juniors bark. Puppies are permitted to growl by indulgent adults, because no threat is involved. Interestingly, dogs do growl at their owners, an indication of the dog's assuming the leadership role.

Wolves howl with all sorts of inflections and meanings; this is their major vocal communicator. The *howl* is used to advertise the territory of the pack, to court, and to summon the group. The assembled pack joins in a chorus of blended notes in obvious enjoyment. Much of this sound effect has been lost in the dog; hounds are the only major dog group in which the howl is preserved, as *baying.* Some breeds apparently are incapable of making the sound, and others do so only rarely.

The *yelp,* on the other hand, is found only in dogs as a means of attracting attention or of indicating submission or pain.

Most dogs have a wider repertoire than indicated here, with assorted sounds of contentment, pleasure, irritation, and so on. There are coos and grumbles, sighs and snorts, mutterings in all tones, varying with the individual dog and its circumstances. You have only to listen to your own dog and encourage its communication.

Nonvocal Communication. The most conspicuous body feature involved in expression is the tail. Its carriage denotes mood as much as any part of the body. Confident and happy dogs carry the tail with an upward swing. A dog uncertain of itself or of a particular situation carries the tail down. When a dog is defeated in a fight or cowed by unfavorable circumstances of life, the tail is tucked between the legs, sometimes to the extent of being plastered against the belly. A dominant animal carries its tail erect. The tail is such a communicator of the dog's feelings that it is regrettable to amputate it, though this is done in a fair number of breeds to meet breeders' standards. Dogs thus deprived still manage to convey a fair amount of expression with what tail is left to them.

One of the most conspicuous features of any animal is its color. Wolves are shaded gray with the back, sides, skull, and tail a dark gray. There are lighter shadings on the paws and muzzle, and beneath the darker areas. The eyes are dark-rimmed with dark lines running back from the eye corners to the ears and ruff of the neck. The ears are dark-edged. Shadings contribute to expression and are therefore a means of communication.

Dogs have a greater variety of colors and patterns. The possible influence that markings may have on communication has not been studied in dogs, but because they do affect behavior in other kinds of animals, including wolves, they probably do so in dogs as well.

Facial expression is dependent on the central features of the head: eyes, ears, and mouth, as well as markings. Expression in the wolf largely depends on the situation (see Chapter 11). These features vary in dogs as a result of selective breeding. In those in which the eyes are more or less hidden by hair, the expression in them is not observable and probably not so effective in communication. Ears, too, convey expression. Erect ears, like the wolf ear, can assume a variety of positions. Dogs with hanging ears have little mobility with them and less variety of ear expressions. Cropped ears, which are artificially erect, are less mobile than naturally erect ones because of the loss of tissue.

Various forms of facial expression are found in canids. The wolf pack leader is aloof, assured, dignified, superior. His (almost always the pack leader is a male) expression and bearing attest to this—he gives the impression of being fully aware of his position and completely in charge. His eyes are his prime communicators. He controls his pack by his penetrating, unblinking gaze. The others lower their heads and do not meet his gaze directly (see Chapter 11). Often, too, there is the worried, insecure member whose shifting gaze gives it the same furtive expression as the shifty-eyed person. It is the "goat" of the pack, picked on by the rest. The puppy, with its soft and innocent expression, is appealing and clearly harmless. It looks gently on all, including the leader, fully and directly in the eyes. An extension of this same expression is found among friendly adult dogs and wolves who look at each other affectionately.

The canine world is one of smells, a world we do not know and barely even suspect. The familiar odors of home and family are learned early. Beyond that, much of canine life consists of investigating scents new since the last checkup and discovering new dogs, new people, and new things. For the dog, with its acutely sensitive nose, the world must be one of undulating patterns of odor, rising and falling, the borders of one area shifting delicately into another.

Smell is the first sense to develop in the puppy; it can locate the teat as soon as it is born. About the eighteenth day, when neither sight nor hearing is well developed, it recognizes its littermates by smell.

COMMUNICATION

Because so much of the dog's world is scent, clearly this sense must be important in communication and behavior.

Leg-lifting in the adult male is the scent communicator most people are aware of. The urine scent informs other dogs, especially males, of the presence of a particular dog. He has claimed the territory as his own and has marked it appropriately. When a dog discovers a urine scent from another dog, he overprints the spot with a few drops of his own urine. Because all adult male dogs follow this practice, there is a great deal of overprinting in an area.

The home is not marked, but the property borders are. That is the dog's notion of its territory, not the property for which its human is taxed. The habit of expanding the territory is brought about by owners' allowing their dogs to anoint an entire neighborhood. It is not necessary for them to do this. Sometimes leg-lifting can occur in the house. It frequently happens with young males reaching sexual maturity, or when an older dog is sexually aroused. It can also happen if a guest dog marks in the house. Handle this quietly (see Chapter 7) and do not punish your dog. Punishment will not correct the situation and may convert a casual accident into a major problem.

Some females also mark territory. They lift a leg but seldom utilize upright objects as does the male. Females in heat and dominant ones also overprint urine of other females.

Some dogs scratch up the earth after excretion. Probably related to spreading the scent, it may be done casually or vigorously, depending on the circumstances. As a conspicuous gesture, it has both visual and scent communication.

Another canine habit associated with smell is rolling in something particularly fragrant. This may be done to put some of that odor on its coat simply because the dog likes the smell and wants to wear it.

One of the prime roles of scent communication is with the dog itself. The body is inspected frequently and washed. A dog that has walked through the muck along a shore will bask in the collection of odors until the scent dissipates before cleaning up.

FRIENDSHIP: YOU AND YOUR DOG

Areas of the body that are most inspected and cleaned are the anal and urinary/genital openings, for the products from them convey information to the dog about itself. Slightly different odors, caused by various foods or drugs, convey information about its current physical state to the dog. We have no idea how it interprets this information.

Because dogs are social creatures, body scents of one individual have meaning to others and affect their behavior. The primary communication scents are the odors in urine and feces, but scents left by paw prints, saliva, and fur also serve that role. Dogs are inordinately interested in excrement, from our point of view. The dog sniffs it to find out whose it is. It can determine the age and sex of the depositor, how recently it was done, and the direction in which that animal was going. It can then follow the scent trail to locate it, if desired. Much information is contained in little product!

The world, as the dog perceives it mentally, must be a scent-image one, very different from the visual-image one we have. Imagery is an important function of the brain in higher animals.

The primary sense for us is sight, and much of the sensory information stored in our brains is visual. We literally "picture a scene." Hearing is also important to us, and we have quite good hearing memory, but we are poorly endowed so far as the sense of smell is concerned. Familiar odors give us mental *pictures* of the scenes associated with the scents. The smell by itself has little meaning. Our very vocabulary illustrates that point. We have many words to describe visual sensations, colors, patterns, appearances, and so on. But we say, "It smells like . . ." to describe odors. This is true of all human languages and cultures. For the dog, though, most imagery is scent-images, with scattered visual and auditory images in the memory scene.

Imagine two friends, dog and human, dozing by a winter's fire, dreaming of their summer dog shows together. They both remember the excitement. In his mind the person pictures the expanses of greenery, the gaily striped tents, the rings, the concessions, and the crowds; the dogs down to the detail of the curve of a stifle, the flow of coat, and the magnificent or flawed performance; his friends, their clothes, and the food. The dog remembering the same scene recalls the new acquaintances smelled, the old ones renewed, the essence of canine everywhere, the smells of grooming sprays, strange foods, tidbits, diverse sweaty and perfumed humans, automotive exhausts, excrement piled or dripping tantalizingly all over the place. Two different views made possible by two different sensory systems and interpretative brains. Our vision sense is better than the dog's, whose scent sense is better than ours. Neither system is really superior to the other, merely different.

Vision is the least important of all the canine senses. Three aspects of vision account for this: acuity and depth perception are not keen, and the dog is color-blind. Since objects are seen only in black, white, and shades of gray with somewhat fuzzy borders, it is to be expected that vision is not a prime sense. An example of visual communication is the control the wolf leader exercises over his pack by eye contact (see Chapter 11). Generally, canines see movement better than mere presence; thus most visual communication is by actions that are at close range and quite apparent. A dog is not even particularly aware of the return of its human after an absence, save by his sounds and scents.

COMMUNICATION AMONG HUMANS

In addition to an understanding of canine communication, you should also know something about human communication in order to communicate effectively with your dog.

We, too, are social beings, and like other social creatures we communicate with our fellows for a variety of purposes. Our interactions are complex. There are some inherent behavioral patterns in humankind, as there are in the canids, but there is also a great deal of learning. Learning begins so early in life that it is difficult to find human behavior uninfluenced by it.

Human communication is discussed here only in the most general terms, emphasizing those aspects that affect communication with the dog.

Vocal Communication. Many animals communicate vocally, but only we are able to put the sounds together to form words and to construct a syntax with those words. Language is the principal way in which human beings communicate their ideas to one another. Although languages differ, the process of language formation and use is universal for humankind. Heredity provides the ability to do this; any specific language is learned. Speech comes naturally to small children who imitate the sounds they hear and learn words, meanings, and techniques to put the parts together to convey their thoughts to others. Listening to youngsters lisp over certain sounds reminds us that this is a learned skill, which takes time to master. It is easy to forget that animals do not have syntactical language; we cannot use human rationality to explain what we want because it has no meaning to them. They cannot be expected to understand us; we must communicate with them in ways that they can understand.

Tone of voice conveys as much about feelings as do the actual words. We seldom think about the tone of our voices, assuming that *what* is said is more important than *how*. Not necessarily. Lovers talk in hushed voices, their gentle tones reflecting the depth of their feelings for which words seem inadequate. The authoritarian voice of the drill sergeant conveys precision by the cadences of his words. The wheedling, whining child signals fatigue more than desire. The woman who screams at her children tells all within earshot about her annoyance, be it with them or life in general. Tone of voice, then, mirrors inner feelings and mood.

In modern social settings, all of us must frequently keep our true feelings bottled up and present a polite and pleasant exterior to the world—that same world which may be presenting us with a lack of security, tensions, or frustrations. One manifestation of tension is the tautness of muscles of the face and vocal apparatus, in turn affecting the timbre of the voice. The words uttered may be pleasant enough, but there is an underlying edgy quality that gives true feelings away. A hard or bitter tone comes into the voice. The person may also be wary, careful with words and tone. When situations reach a peak of irritation and frustration and the person feels ready to explode, the words are frequently obscene and hateful, the tone belligerent. A person's strident emotions, more than a strident mind, may be dictating the verbal responses that are made.

We usually think of laughter as pure pleasure, yet often it has a mocking quality and frequently someone is the object of amusement. Laughing over shared jokes and experiences is an activity that helps bind a group together. The outsider inevitably feels apart from them and may suspect that they are deriding him. Laughter conveys emotions that are quite different from smiles. One evidence for that is that dogs relate favorably to a human smile, but they do not like to be laughed at.

Nonvocal Communication. So much of our communication with other people is verbal that we tend to assume that this is the only way we communicate. Body language, for the most part, is subconscious and conveys feelings and mood rather than ideas. We often project more than we might consciously wish to.

Behavioral studies done on people of different cultures indicate that there are fundamental similarities in facial expressions, use of hands, and other body movements. These reflect a common use of the body as a communications system. We "know" how to communicate this way; it is built into our makeup to do so and is, therefore, instinctive as it is in canids.

All sorts of body movements serve as communicators. Aside from shrugging the shoulders, most people are unaware of the amount of body language they use. The simple yes/no head movements are universal gestures. Turning the head away is a sign of rejection used from infancy. Nodding indicates agreement and may convey appeasement or submission. The standing human figure betrays emotions very well. When the person is tense or irritated, the muscles are tensed, movements are abrupt, and the body is stiffly erect, almost as if it were propped up. A restive person moves about aimlessly or, if unable to do so, fidgets, fiddling with his body or some object, unable to be still. In relaxation the body may be erect, though not stiffly so, or it may slump against some support.

Hands can be extremely expressive. Although some gestures are cultural and learned, many are instinctive. The hand extended palm up is a sign of begging used by the child, by the beggar, and as a symbolic gesture for entreaty or pleading. The index finger points to show location and to indicate emphasis. The arm extended with upraised hand signals the observer to stop and to come no closer. The arm held up with upraised and shaking fist screams defiance. Arms flung outward invite an embrace; an arm or hand gesturing inward toward the body is a signal to come closer. When speaking, many people use their hands extensively to describe scenes, events, and participants. The halt signal then means negation or rejection, whereas the gesture to come signifies collection or possession. Gestures may be friendly, as a light touch to the hand, or intimidating, as when the speaker grabs at the listener or the intervening space in order to press home a point.

Facial expression is another form of nonvocal communication. The face is the focus of human communication. Faces are mobile, the expression in them shifting from moment to moment in accordance with sensory information, thoughts, and mood, usually subconsciously. Some faces are highly mobile, alive with changing moods; others less so, even wearing a mask of inscrutability. Observers tend to be uncomfortable with this expression because they cannot "read" the person's mood.

Creases develop in the skin in relation to underlying facial structures and use and are typically found on the forehead and around the eyes and mouth. Individual variations are caused by differences in skin elasticity, the amount of time spent in sun and wind, and the frequency of certain expressions. The human face reveals a great deal about character.

The eyes are particularly important in human communication. In ordinary conversation, a person does not stare into the eyes of the person to whom he is speaking, but glances at them from time to time, as if checking to be sure the listener really is listening, then glances away to check the scenery or to watch others. It is as if the eyes had a life of their own. Eye expression is affected by their setting and brows as much as by the eyes themselves and influences the actions of others as it does in canids. A penetrating gaze directly to the eyes is intimidating and is employed to dominate. A person who is uncertain or uncomfortable looks aside, unable to raise his eyes to the other's face. Many women, well aware of the role of the eyes, especially with men, enhance them for effect. Glasses also accentuate the eyes. Heavy or dark-rimmed ones draw attention to the eyes more than rimless ones do; the choice is probably influenced, at least subconsciously, by the desire to accentuate the eyes.

Dominance and subordination occur in humans as they do in the canids (see Chapter 11) and are clearly communicated by various means. The urge to dominate is strong—considerably stronger in humans than in the canids, which try for dominance but readily accept a subordinate role. Human beings, with their intellectual capabilities, seethe at inequities and plan to redress them by some sort of action. Human societies, being infinitely more complex than canine society, present different occasions for dominance. Although it is common for a person to be dominant in one context and subordinate in another, some individuals will dominate any setting they are in. Others are always subordinates. Knowledge and skill aid dominance and are involved in the notion of "getting ahead" by means of an education. In humans, as in canines, subordinates announce the fact by lowering their bodies in relation to that of the dominant person, for example, sitting to listen to the standing leader speak or bowing before rulers.

All human groups develop leaders, and even groups of subordinates have their more dominant members who take over the leadership. There is a great deal of jockeying for dominance in human societies.

Humans, not possessing an impressive coat of fur, have more than made up for the deficiency by covering their bodies. Clothes do far more than keep one warm; literally, clothes make the person. The style, the colors, the attendant decorations, often in sparkling metals, call attention to the person in overt or subtle ways. Clearly, some people are more aware of this feature than others, but we all recognize it, at least subconsciously. Shy and "mousy" types do not choose flamboyant colors and styles, nor do confident and gregarious people wear unrelieved grays and tans. As individuality shows through in our choice of clothing, so does the effect of society. We dress for the particular society and occasion. Teenage conformity is notorious, but hardly unique.

In human societies, the leader (usually male) is the impressive person whose eminence is granted by virtue of who and what he is. He carries himself with appropriate regal bearing. He dresses the part. He has the cooperative respect or fearful adherence of the society's subordinates. His position is not secure; he has it as long as he can maintain it against those who are only too eager to supplant him. Power plays are a constant feature of all human societies.

Aggression is clearly a human attribute with, apparently, a base in heredity. Infants show strong tendencies along this line, crying angrily, striking out with hands and feet, or grabbing objects. Small children have outbursts of temper in which they assail other children, other creatures, and inanimate objects quite violently. There is a lot of body language associated with aggressiveness. Color drains from the face and the person goes "white with rage." The mouth is dry. Eyebrows knit a deep frown; the eyes, appearing to burn with intensity, stare straight ahead; the lips are compressed into hard, thin lines; cheeks are tense. The expression is fierce. The person draws himself up to full height, tall, tense, and impressive; the chest expands; arms are held out rigidly with clenched fists; feet are apart, ready to move. The person is not to be trifled with. He means business and is ready to act. Actual fights do not necessarily result from aggressive encounters; frequently they are resolved by words alone.

Aggression should not be thought of as an entirely negative attribute, however. Assertiveness, one manifestation of aggression, is an important component of personality. Because we have the capacity to see the consequences of our acts, we should be able to control and rechannel our aggressiveness in more positive directions. Working with animals is one way of doing so.

Of all the variety of human facial expressions, only two—the friendly and the disapproving expressions—will be discussed. These are the ones that we use most with our dogs.

The friendly expression is an inviting and approachable one. The mouth is relaxed; the lips are open, pulled back and up at the corners; the cheeks are raised, forming crinkles at the outer corners of the eyes, which look ahead directly. The expression is sparkly, smiling, and inviting. The smile, trademark of our kind, is a unique human expression, a universal sign of friendliness, whose meaning transcends language barriers worldwide. Used by persons in authority (parents, teachers, doctors, political leaders), it signifies support and reassurance. The small child's smile is a disarming one. Each child learns early what the smile means, what it can bring, and how to employ it; a skill that is never lost.

The expression of displeasure contrasts sharply with the friendly face. The lips are compressed in a thin line of determination or extended in a pout. The outer corners of the mouth turn down. Cheeks are lowered, flattening out the wrinkles around the eyes and making the face appear drawn out; they may be rigidly set or quivering with tension. The forehead is compressed in a frown, lowering the brows and bringing the eyes closer together. The expression in the eyes is hard and uninviting, conveying annoyance and unfriendliness. In con-

THE DOG'S-EYE VIEW OF HUMAN BODY LANGUAGE.

This person is relaxed in a casual slouch, and his expression, if not smiling, is kindly and definitely approachable.

But here he is displeased. His stance and expression are aggressive and threatening. One would hesitate to approach.

trast with the friendly expression, which makes one wish to approach, the displeased expression makes one hesitate to get close or wish to withdraw. The responses to these expressions are the same for both dogs and people.

The body language is mixed. His stance is as aggressive as previously, but he is trying to cover up his feelings by a fake smile. No dog is fooled by that expression (see Chapter 5, "Mixed Signals").

4

Social Behavior

Dogs are social creatures. When they live under natural conditions, their behavior is remarkably similar to that of wolves; both live in a structured social organization, the pack, presided over by a leader (see Chapter 11). However, in the usual setting, where dogs live with people, they form a social group together. The dog's natural social behavior is still present, though sometimes adapted to the situation of domestication.

SOME EXAMPLES OF SOCIAL BEHAVIOR

Social Greeting. For a social animal, greeting one's fellows and making new acquaintances is an important part of life. When two dogs of the same sex meet for the first time, they approach with uplifted tails gently wafting and stretch forward to measure each other's scent. If relations are cordial, they come closer and sniff each other about the face and ears, and along the body to the attractive scent areas of the rear. In wolves, the leader does the sniffing and displays himself to be sniffed. The subordinate stands quietly, allowing itself to be sniffed, then almost reticently sniffs the leader. With dogs, the older animal assumes the lead and the younger is more submissive. Two equals display and sniff and may then follow this up with an aggressive confrontation to establish their relative positions (see Chapter 11). If the greeters are of opposite sexes, reactions are different. The male frequently makes advances to the female if she is attractive to him, whether or not she is in heat. His sniffing is more persistent, his tail wags faster, and he may use other amorous gestures, such as nuzzling, pawing, or cooing. If she is not ready to breed, the female does not put up with this sort of conduct and snarls and snaps at him. He respects her enough not to answer with aggression—male dogs do not fight females—but not necessarily enough to stop his attentions until her savagery finally discourages him.

Many owners, not appreciating the importance of social life or the normal manifestations of greetings, condemn their dogs to lives without canine contacts. This is unkind to a social animal. It is better to be discriminating, limiting the dog's social

These two young dogs are meeting for the first time. The more dominant dog stands taller, with uplifted tail.

life to those animals that are compatible and healthy. This provides an enjoyable aspect to the dog's life.

Solicitation. When young puppies nurse, they paw at the breast in a rhythmic, kneading fashion, alternating forepaws. Pawing, as well as sucking, aids milk release. Toward the end of the nursing period, the mother stands, forcing the pups to stand or sit in order to reach the nipples. Although this is good for the muscles of the back and neck, coordination is not yet good enough to permit the use of both forepaws for kneading, as is possible when the pups are lying down. But the urge remains, so one paw is used to bat the breast while the other maintains balance.

The puppy learns that pawing brings gratification, and it persists as a habit all of the dog's life. Pawing is used as a sign of affection, in courtship, and as a gesture of apology, appeal, or submission.

Nuzzling is another form of solicitation. The puppy burrows into its mother's belly in search of the nipple. It is rewarded by milk.

In wolves, the pups mob their parents and other pack members on their return from hunting, climbing all over them and nuzzling and licking at their lips and mouth. Their behavior elicits the vomit reflex. The puppy then learns that its act of begging is rewarded by food. Even after the puppies pass the stage of needing to have their food predigested for them, the mobbing, jumping, and nuzzling responses continue and are used as social greetings when pack members return to the group. Most dogs do not get the chance to practice this method of weaning (see Chapter 2). The puppies are fed while the mother is absent. However, they have the same greeting pattern and climb all over her when she returns, but, not being hungry, they do not solicit vigorously enough to bring forth the vomiting reflex.

Some puppy solicitation behaviors persist into adulthood because they still produce gratification. It is the *nature* of the gratification that changes. Mobbing a returning dog is common. It is greeted by nuzzling with the muzzle thrust into the neck or face fur, accompanied by sniffling and snorting sounds and happy tail wagging. Jumping on people is this same sort of social greeting. The dog attempts to nuzzle the face affectionately, as instinct and experience dictate, while barking and wagging joyfully.

Several other puppy responses are carried over into adulthood. The universal canid habit of lying on the back as a sign of submission begins when tiny puppies roll over for their mother's attention. Because the behavior was originally associated with excretion, it is not surprising that a pup may urinate in that situation. It gets over the habit quickly if it is ignored, but if you scold or make a fuss over the act, the dog is likely to keep on doing this all of its life. Another holdover from puppyhood solicitation is the dog's habit of cleaning up after itself when it vomits. Your proper response is either to ignore the cleanup or to move the dog away from the scene and quietly clean it up yourself.

Social Grooming. Dogs not only attend to their own grooming, but they may also groom their fellows as an act of friendship or affection. Social grooming also begins in puppyhood with the mother's washing her pups. Her primary interest is the anus and urinary/genital openings, but many females take on the whole pup as well. They may routinely clean the pups after they have eaten, sloppily, from a dish. They may even take on pups other than their own. Grooming may be done to adults as well, and the act seems the prerogative of older members of the group. One of my males washed the insides of the ears of his females and youngsters, who reacted with expressions of pleasure and contentment. In my experience, grooming is only done by a senior or dominant dog.

Copying. Young wolves learn the routine of the pack by observation, and so do dogs. It is always easiest to bring a young

These two dogs are special friends. Grooming is done by the more dominant dog.

puppy into a house with adult dogs because it learns appropriate conduct from them and simply falls in step. Dogs also copy human actions. Copying may be not so much a form of flattery as the desire to join in whatever is going on. One of my dogs picks berries with me. She has developed some skill over the years, adroitly plucking the ripe ones and even spitting out leaves or unripe ones inadvertently picked. She also copies whistling and singing by howling. Encouraged in her musical endeavors, she howls in response to "A-woooo" from me or "Sing to me" said in a singsong voice. My other dogs observe this and sometimes join in, but they have never done so spontaneously.

Play. Only the higher social animals play. Although play is, as often described, a preparation for life, it is more than that alone. Play is the natural learning situation for the puppy and helps to develop temperament and personality. It is also fun. Although it is most often associated with puppyhood, it need not be limited to it.

One of the nicest ages in the life of the dog is when it first begins to play. When puppies are about three weeks old, with

First beginnings of play in 21-day-old puppies.

their senses fully developed, they begin to interact. The puppy wants to touch its fellows, and it does so by nuzzling and nudging, filling its nostrils with their essence, and by pawing and nibbling. Soon thereafter, something else is born into that infant brain—the sense of deviltry. It is first seen as a faintly wicked gleam of eye, a look not seen in those baby eyes before. Not only must the puppy touch its fellows, it must bat at them, it must lunge, it must grab at a passing tail, it must stalk and pounce. It plays. It learns that its fumbly gestures are answered in kind, pounce for pounce, nibble for nibble. The puppies roll about, exploring one another's bodies and reactions. It's fun. Play is the first social interaction of the new little social creature.

The games puppies play are all physical encounters. Fighting games are scuffles in which the pups rush at each other, attack, topple, roll, growl, and bite. There is nothing serious going on, no one is hurt, but the sounds are fierce. Sex games involve investigation of the genital areas of all the pups and general mounting. These are pack games in which everyone participates, but without any concerted group action. The pups try out their needle-sharp teeth on everything: one another, humans, mother, their bed, toys. They play with objects and

Two young juveniles playing.

contest the possession of them with tug-of-war games. They can follow a ball and may carry objects. They are exceedingly curious and interested in everything that is going on.

Both dogs and wolves bow as an invitation to play. The front end is lowered, the rear up with the tail high and waving, the facial expression eager, almost laughing. All of the body communicators entice. There are short, sharp barks; pawing at the ground; leaping at the other in a carefree fashion; sometimes standing on the hind legs to embrace or box at each other. The dog uses these same tactics with people.

Dominance. During the fourth to fifth week, something else appears in the sheer fun of play. A serious note has been subtly introduced. Evidence of a power play begins to surface. Someone is a bit bigger, a bit stronger, a bit more forward. This pup, on its own assertiveness discovered in play, begins to take over and manage the group. The others may allow this, or there may be struggles in which it wrests leadership from the competition. By the seventh week, the litter's leader has been determined. Although that pup takes over the litter, it is always submissive to any adults. Leadership in all-male or mixed-sex litters usually goes to the most assertive male, which is usually also the largest; in all-female litters, it goes to another assertive individual, the noisiest. There may be a definite hierarchy below the leader, or all may form a group of more or less equals below the leader.

Mother's Teachings. Where dogs are raised under natural conditions, play also involves other family members playing with the litter. Generally, dog litters are more isolated, with the puppies never meeting their father and having only limited time with

Dominance and submission in two adult females. Lowered posture is typical of the more submissive dog.

the mother after weaning. This is not the best learning situation for the puppies. The mother should be with her pups for learning and discipline while the litter is still together. She will play with them, allowing them to climb all over her and attack her in their bumbling, puppy ways. Indulgent elders do the same. Pups learn best from adults when they have gone too far, or the game has gone on long enough. Mother should be allowed to take her children places and introduce them to the scents of her world. They will happily stumble after her as she strides purposefully along a known path. They will neither stray nor get lost; she sees to that. And if they encounter something fearful, they have only to be with her to find the security they need.

5

Building the Bond

Up to this point, we have considered the ways in which dogs and humans communicate among themselves. We now need to consider the ways in which we communicate with our dogs.

In our relationship with our dogs, there must be no question of roles. This is no democracy! You are the leader; your dog is the follower. At the same time, this is not a dictatorship or a master-slave relationship. It is the friendship of two separate beings: a wise and kindly leader and a respectful and willing follower.

The human is the one who raises the dog, molds its character, teaches it to conform to his ways—not the other way around. There are dog-run households, with the humans in dancing attendance on the whims of the dog. That is not what you want. The proper relationship was not established in the first place when the dog was young, usually through a lack of knowledge. The purpose of this book is to help you establish that good relationship, rather than inadvertently creating problems that have to be corrected later on. It is so much easier to raise the dog right, building the bond of friendship from the start of your life together.

FRIENDSHIP: YOU AND YOUR DOG

TOGETHERNESS

In order to build a relationship, the dog and its person must be together. Obviously, this is not possible twenty-four hours a day, 365 days a year; you do have other commitments. But the dog should be part of the family, included in many activities, and also have some special attention and training. This gives the dog a sense of worth and individuality. It is particularly important if yours is a situation in which the dog is left alone for long periods of time each day. If you do something special with your dog when you return, it eagerly anticipates this time and is more apt to be content while you are away.

Togetherness is sharing. It is doing things together: a run on a beach at sunrise, a visit with human and canine friends, training, a walk. It is doing nothing together: sitting on a step watching the world's work go on, dozing on a lazy afternoon, passing a quiet evening with your dog napping beside your chair. It is learning to know each other's idiosyncrasies and how to live with them. It is the pleasure of one another's company.

The bond between you builds in togetherness.

COMMUNICATING WITH YOUR DOG

Conversation. Companionable conversation is just plain talking to the dog in a friendly, chatty fashion. The dog is not called on to do anything, nor need it pay much attention. The familiar voice provides a pleasant background music, acknowledged by an interested look and a wagging tail. Sometimes, it may even be helpful to you to talk to a patient and undemanding listener!

Commands. Commands are short, snappy directives to the dog. They are attention arresters that call for a response. There are four aspects of giving commands to a dog. First, the actual words are single-syllable ones, usually one word, sometimes two. They are words that have a certain punch to the sound and good carrying quality (see Appendix 3). A second aspect of the command is its tone. There should be an authoritative ring to the voice. It should be pleasant but firm. This is where your concept of dogs and training, as well as your mood, really shows. If you think of training as coercion, if you have something to prove and use the dog as a means of doing so, or if you are in a poor emotional state, then the tone is hard, the commands barked out. Underlying the tone is the implied threat "Do this or else." Just as bad is wheedling, nagging, or requesting. Dogs are extremely tone-perceptive and respond to tone of voice more than to the actual words. The third aspect of a command is its volume, which should only be loud enough to get the dog's attention. Fourth, commands should be consistent; the same word is always used for the same act.

Commands mean something very specific—they are not idle chatter. No dog will carry out a command automatically; it must be shown what to do or put into a position *while* the command is given and then praised. In time, when it learns to

Togetherness is doing nothing together.

associate the word with the act, it will obey. It also must be taught that commands are always to be obeyed, an association that requires consistency in training. The dog's voluntary compliance, not compulsion, is desired; dogs respect authority and readily comply, provided they know what is expected. It is up to you to create conditions so that the dog will want to obey you.

Body language is an important type of command. Therefore, nonvocal commands are used with vocal ones in teaching the dog, thus training it to respond to both words and signals.

The elements of commands, then, are the following: crisp words, a pleasant yet authoritative voice, the lowest possible volume, consistency, a respected leader, and a willing follower.

Praise. Praise is approval. It confirms that what the dog did is what you wanted it to do. It is encouragement of the dog's hesitant and faltering attempts to understand and to do your bidding. It is a reward for correct behavior. Rewards have several forms. To the dog in tune with its human after years of association, a smile, a kind word, or a light touch is sufficient. That is hardly enough encouragement for the learner, however. In that case, you must communicate your pleasure with all your faculties: the friendly, smiling face; a light and happy voice; words of praise, petting, and sometimes great huzzahs and hugs (see Chapter 3). Words should have sounds that can be drawn out and that the dog learns to associate with approval: "Goood boy," "Awwwright," "Wheee." Genuine enthusiasm is the key, not duration. Food can also be used as a reward. It is best used as a motivator and not overused to the point that the dog depends on it or tends to respond for food rather than the joy of pleasing you.

Timing is crucial to praise. It must be done *as* the dog is doing what is wanted, or immediately afterward. The longer the time gap between the act and the praise, especially in learning something new, the more difficult it is for the dog to make the association.

Sincere praise forges the bond of friendship.

A puppy needs lots of enthusiastic praise and cuddling.

Discipline. The word *discipline* is often used incorrectly as a synonym for *punishment.* Punishment implies retribution for a crime. Discipline, on the other hand, is training to instill self-control, obedience, and acceptance of authority, or to correct errors.

Discipline is disapproval. It tells the dog that what it did was incorrect or not acceptable. You are displeased; you look that way and speak that way (see Chapter 3). Typically, the dog tries to ingratiate itself with its person and not to provoke annoyance, but it takes a while before the dog makes the association between its actions and your reaction and realizes that you are not pleased with what it has done. Discipline helps make that association.

Timing is as crucial to discipline as it is to praise. It should be administered *as* the dog is in the process of doing something wrong or immediately afterward. Always use the mildest discipline that brings results. Keep your voice low and level. Aim to reach the point where only a subdued "No" or a disapproving glance is sufficient. It takes time to reach that level of rapport.

As you get to know your dog, you become more certain of the reasons for the undesirable behavior and can gauge discipline accordingly. Clearly, there is a difference between the dog who doesn't know what is expected or is tired and the one who isn't paying attention or is trying to avoid doing something. Sensitive or well-trained dogs sense disapproval by body language, a frown, withholding of praise, or a regretful "Oh, no," but those reactions do not work with dominant, headstrong, or untrained dogs. Curt words uttered in a sharp or disgusted tone of voice emphatically convey displeasure: "Ah-ah," "No," "Stop it." The slip collar and lead are effective disciplinary devices commonly used in dog training (see Chapter 8).

If more stringent measures are needed, they should follow the natural disciplinary tactics used in canid societies (see Chapter 11). Following the example of the pack leader who disciplines pups by shaking them, grab the scruff of the neck and give a quick shake. Act swiftly to capitalize on the element

For the well-trained dog, discipline can be administered by words and body language. Recognizing the disapproval, she looks aside.

of surprise and shake strongly enough to make the pup squeal. For this, the tiny puppy of a toy breed needs only to be plucked by thumb and forefinger, whereas the stocky pup of a large breed requires both hands and may need to be lifted slightly so that the forefeet are just off the ground for a moment. In keeping with natural discipline, you must show no animosity, rejection, or nagging afterward. As soon as the desired behavior is achieved, praise the pup.

If you need still stronger tactics, use the shake-up and scold the dog while looking it fully in the face. As the message comes across, the dog will look aside.

Another procedure that works well is to use canid pinning tactics. Drop the dog onto its back and hold it there until it becomes limp. Words are not used; speed and surprise are. These two strong measures should only be employed on dogs that disobey established patterns of conduct and do not respond to lesser measures. Success is important; therefore be

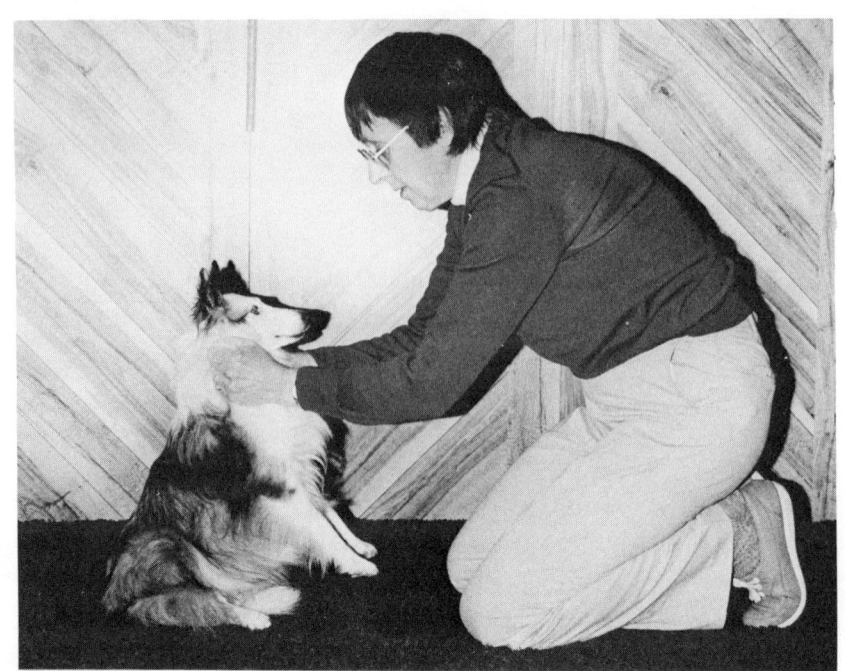

The shake-up is a stronger form of discipline. The dog's forelegs are lifted slightly; she is held in position and scolded. Eye contact is important.

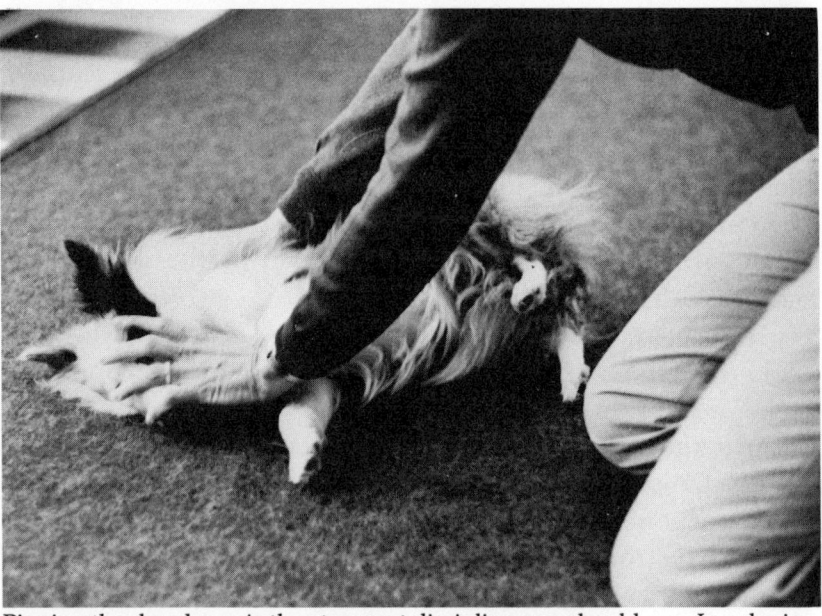

Pinning the dog down is the strongest discipline you should use. In submission, the dog lifts her hind leg and pulls her tail in against her belly.

This dog has just been mildly disciplined. Her body language, folded-back ears and outstretched paw, are gestures of ingratiation. The person's relaxed posture, smile, and kind words indicate acceptance. There are no hard feelings.

sure that you are physically able to administer this level of discipline before trying it.

Only minimal physical corrections should be used with a puppy because of the possibility of injuring a body not fully developed. Sensitive puppies can be corrected with "No"; more rambunctious ones may also require some shaking. A young pup that bites or chews can be corrected by tapping the side of the muzzle firmly with a couple of fingers, or, if the puppy is persistent, by a quick smack *under* the chin. If you strike on the top of the face, the dog will duck its head, not only blunting the force of the correction but also learning to cringe or cower when a hand comes over its head ("hand-shy"). Correctly raised puppies should not need any of the stronger measures when mature.

Harsh discipline should be reserved for extreme situations such as a dog fight or an attack on a person.

Always follow any type of correction with praise. You are, thus, rewarding your dog for no longer doing the act for which you corrected it.

The Lead as a Communicator. The usual apparel for the dog is a collar and lead. The lead attaches the dog to its human, as required by many municipalities, and also serves as a communication link between them.

The dog that has been trained to walk properly on lead walks with its human in the very picture of togetherness. By contrast, the untrained dog is out for a romp, the human tags along, and the lead continually gets snarled up in them and the various impediments of the area. The person grabs at the lead to rein in the dog, which bounds along on its merry way. That lead is a nuisance, not a communicator.

Although the lead has a wrist loop, there is no control exerted unless it is also clutched by hand. As it is primarily hand-held, the amount of muscle tautness in the shoulders and arms is directly communicated to the dog through the lead. Tension and nervousness tend to make you grip the lead tightly, but when you are relaxed, there is little pressure on it.

Tightness of the lead is communicated to the dog as a tightening of the collar around its neck, exerting pressure on the neck and throat. Loosening and tightening are used as an effective training device (see Chapter 8).

The lead communicates the trainer's mood. Lightly held, it indicates confidence and trust. But used to pull the dog around or as a whip, it expresses a domineering attitude. This creates a threatening situation for the dog, who then reacts according to its temperament by becoming sullen and resentful or fearful and cowering.

The lead is a tool for handling a dog and a link between two sentient beings. When properly trained, the dog responds to the slightest lead tension by looking up to see what its human wants. The lead, then, communicates togetherness and security.

This is a good example of poor lead handling and poor communication between person and dog. The grip on the lead is so tight that the knuckles show, and the slip collar is pulled taut around the dog's neck. The muscles of the shoulders, back, and face are tense. The dog responds to all this by pulling back and away from the person. She lowers her body submissively and looks up anxiously. Compare this with the picture of good handling in Chapter 8 (p. 103).

Mixed Signals. When all of our communicators (facial expression, tone of voice, and body language) are not in agreement because of internal conflicts, the communication signals are mixed.

When you are tense, tired, or irritated, all of your movements are stiffer than when you are relaxed. Your facial expression is set, your voice edgy or cross, your shoulder and arm muscles tensed, your actions abrupt. The pat you give your dog is a perfunctory one. Picking up all these clues, your dog realizes that something is amiss with you. If you are consciously making an effort to be *nice,* you are apt to put on a fake smile and be pseudojolly. Your signals are mixed. Confused, the dog is not quite sure which signals to respond to: the reassuring voice or the almost aggressive stance and displeased expression. Trying to cope with both, the dog loses its concentration and does poorly. You become exasperated and impatient. Everything falls apart! This is not the way to communicate with your dog.

Vocal mixed signals are given by some people who are otherwise fairly consistent in body language. Their voices shift from pleading to demanding to scolding to panic in rapid succession. This is extremely confusing to the dog, with its acute ability to distinguish tones.

Self-Control. You must be in control of yourself when training your dog. To give your dog confidence in you, you must have a firm resolve and gentle hands. You must be a kind, fair, and consistent person.

No one, of course, is absolutely consistent, but you should aim for consistency and try to avoid wide swings of mood that are good for neither you nor your dog. Those who are most successful with dogs have an "animal sense." They are knowledgeable and able to communicate and have quite predictable actions. Their very predictability gives the animal the sense of security and confidence that makes the best basis for building a good relationship.

Most of us fall short of this ideal because of personality, health, and the emotional pressures of our lives. The person is the key element in training the dog. You must know yourself. You may become more aware of yourself, your irritation levels, and your responses to them in working with your dog than in human associations. In part, at least, this is due to the greater complexity of human relations compared to the simplicity and straightforward relationship with a dog.

Most instructors of training classes advise their human students to work with their dogs every day. The advantage of daily work is the formation of habits through frequent repetition, which facilitates learning (see Chapter 6). But there are times to refrain from training, even for several days. If the conditions of life have reached a pressure-cooker stage, you are not in a good emotional state to train. Communications signals are mixed or may be uniformly bad. Because they are more sensitive to body movements than people are, dogs tend to become surly, sullen, unruly, or fearful if they have to work for long with someone who is inconsistent or confusing. Whenever you feel unable to cope with training in the proper spirit, don't do it. Take a walk with your dog to help defuse your pent-up feelings; then play or just relax together. There always is another day.

6

Learning to Learn

The seven-week-old puppy has a fully developed brain capable of learning. Indeed, it has been learning as its brain has developed. It has experienced the physical world through its senses. It has developed certain behaviors as it has interacted with its littermates, mother, and any other animals with which it has associated. It has also learned something about people, knowing them, we hope, only as sources of affection, attention, and pleasant experiences. By the time the average puppy goes to its new home, it has learned a great deal but is still in a relatively unformed state as far as its personality and behavior are concerned. These are mostly shaped by later events.

The youngster, typically, is eager, friendly, happy, and loving. It is ready to learn and does, whether or not you teach it. The pup should be taught to do some things, not to do others, and to obey willingly and happily. As it learns and matures, the puppy gains in confidence and poise. To achieve this, you must have definite expectations of the dog and know how to obtain them. This requires skill in understanding and communication—not merely forcing the dog to do your bidding.

HOW THE DOG LEARNS

Essentially, the dog lives in a physical world. The dog receives information about the world from its senses. It makes decisions about appropriate actions to take and stores information in the brain in the form of memory. Gradually, perceptions and responses are built into behavioral patterns that become fixed, so that a repeated event, circumstance, or sensation evokes a particular response. Fixed behaviors, then, become conditioned responses or habits.

Association. Dogs learn by association. Certain events are pleasant in themselves or bring pleasure as the result of associated sensations. Others are unpleasant or uncomfortable. The dog, like any other animal, prefers the pleasant and avoids the unpleasant. This natural preference is used in training. A desired response is rewarded by praise; one that is not wanted is discouraged by correction. As long as the distinction is clear to the dog, it will try to do what is wanted. It does so, not only to seek the pleasant and to avoid the unpleasant, but also because of its inherent loyalty to its leader and its desire to please him.

Repetition. Dogs learn by repetition. As experiences recur, the dog's responses to them become established. Training, then, requires repetition in order to fix the appropriate response.

For example, the dominance order in a litter is established by association and repetition. The larger, more inquisitive, and outgoing puppy takes the lead. It asserts itself with its littermates, and if it finds them less assertive, it pushes itself until it becomes the dominant pup in the litter. The more hesitant puppies learn that they will be pushed around and nipped and will have food stolen. Gradually, they learn to be more retiring.

Problem Solving. Dogs learn problem solving by trial and error and insight learning. A tied dog learns to avoid snubbing the line and pulling itself up short by *trial-and-error* learning. *Insight learning,* the ability to solve problems mentally, is a type of thinking. It requires experience first, making it usually a characteristic of mature animals. Dogs used in service—for the handicapped, on guard, on the farm, or in the field—almost continuously show insight into the diverse problems of their jobs.

Abstract Thought. Dogs are not capable of abstract thought. They do not learn by explanation, neither do they act from a sense of morality or ethics. It is, therefore, not possible to teach dogs by appealing to their sense of rightness. That may seem to contradict the numerous examples of canine acts of kindness, bravery, and empathy toward humans and other animals. More likely, these actions are part of the endowment of intelligent, social animals. Canid pack members are interdependent but also affectionate and loyal toward one another. They have a social consciousness that makes such acts possible without morality. That awareness may well be the forerunner of the still higher level of consciousness on which human societies have based their moral codes.

THE TRAINING PROCESS

Because the dog is essentially physically, not intellectually, oriented, training is also physical. The dog is placed into a position gently *while* being given a command, and, as this is repeated, it comes to associate the word with the action. It receives praise for correct action and discipline for incorrect action. When praise and correction are associated with the puppy's acts in a clear-cut manner, they aid in making the association between word and action in the dog's mind.

Commands are the directives you give that call for a definite response by the dog. The timing of praise and discipline is crucial. Always do them *as* the dog is doing the act in question, or *immediately* thereafter (see Chapter 5).

The distinction between praise and correction must be sharp. A lukewarm tone of voice in which commands, praise, and corrections are given in the same monotone simply confuses the dog. Although tone is very important, volume is not. Yelling indicates that you are not in control, and dogs learn to disregard it. Explanations of misdeeds nag, and the dog learns to ignore them or becomes resentful of the nagging. Attempts to shame a dog into, or out of, doing something are ineffective because the dog lacks value judgments to apply to its acts. It must simply learn to do what you want: the reasons are beyond the dog.

Learning requires concentration. Young puppies, with their short attention spans, can concentrate for only a few moments at a time; this gradually improves with maturity and learning. Never overdo training. Do not ask your dog to repeat any activity more than three times—there is always another day. Always start with a fresh, well-rested dog and stop before its enthusiasm peters out. You, too, should be rested and not tense or irritable.

Learning is a bit-by-bit process. A particular activity is broken down into a series of small steps, taken up one at a time. When the first step has been learned, the next is undertaken, so that there is a progressive buildup to the complete activity. Although that may sound straightforward, the problem comes in determining *when* something has been learned. The usual indicators are that the task is done correctly each time it is asked for over a period of several days. But real learning may not have occurred yet, and the dog may backslide later. This simply indicates that the first lesson was not completely mastered, and training must back up to ensure that it is. Distractions confuse the issue for a dog. It may have learned a lesson and be able to repeat it as long as the conditions (location, people, noise, and so on) remain the same, but be unable to do so in different conditions. Although the dog is probably unsure of itself, it is important to insist, gently but firmly, that the lesson proceed, for that discipline is the best security the dog can have.

Variety in training sessions is needed to provide mental flexibility and prevent boredom for both of you. Sometimes new activities are introduced and old ones reviewed. Other times, there is only a review, or only a new activity. A special outing is enough education for a particular day.

When all the lessons of Chapters 7 and 8 have been taught, repeat them, and in different locations, to fix the responses in the dog's mind. *This* is what makes a well-trained dog. Then add imaginative activities and tricks of your own.

As the more knowledgeable of the partnership, you must accept responsibility for your dog's failure to act according to acceptable conduct. Dogs are not deceitful. They are often confused or inconsistent or seem to be doing the wrong thing deliberately. This failure to respond correctly may be due to a lack of understanding or concentration, unintentional training, fear, or a lack of a good working relationship. All of these problems rest squarely with you. You must always have control of yourself and the situation. Keep your expectations realistic and do not push the dog to achieve faster than its ability to absorb what you are teaching. To do their best, dogs need brief training sessions in unpressured settings, with a person who is consistent, firm, and patient.

PUPPIES ARE SPECIAL

In General. Early experiences are important in shaping the dog's perceptions of humans. It should regard them as friendly creatures with whom it would like to associate. Inheritance determines basic responses, thus making some dogs more outgoing, others more reserved, and still others shy or fearful. Heredity is not a rigid determiner, however, and experiences early in life have a strong influence in shaping personality and subsequent behavior.

A healthy canine temperament is an easygoing, rough-and-tumble one. Delicate or aggressive temperaments are, in most cases, made that way by the treatment the dog receives when it is young and impressionable. The dog's personality, much less flexible than a person's, is solidly shaped by inheritance and early experiences. Later experiences, even unfavorable ones, do not have nearly so great an impact. Temperament and personality are set, for *life*, during the critical time from three to sixteen weeks of age. In order to have a good relationship, you must see that they are well set.

The relation of the dog to its human is that of a subordinate toward a leader. The leader leads by determining who does what, when, and how. A good one is wise, kindly, and respected. Initially, the puppy's relationship to its human is one of need: for food, protection, security, and companionship. In a good relationship, respect develops later, then affection, then adoration. The dog's leader is its god. It is very hard for a mere human to be in *that* role—slips do occur, but the dog can take them in stride as long as the general tenor of the situation is supportive. Ideally, every dog should have the sort of human it can adore.

Those who are indifferent, or vary inconsistently from overly soft to overly harsh, or who are cruel lose the dog's respect. Its attitude and behavior become as poor as its person's. They may tolerate one another, but there is no joy in the relationship for either.

As soon as you acquire your puppy, begin training it. You have three objectives: to develop temperament and personality, to teach the skills needed to live in human society, to have the puppy enjoy the learning process. Keep these in mind at all times.

Be friendly, encouraging, and supportive. Use a gentle hand and a happy voice. Talk with your puppy almost all of the time you are training in order to help it concentrate on you. Praise the puppy for trying; praise it for being in the right position even though you put it there. Keep your voice low when praising, or you will excite your puppy into forgetting.

Use words, cuddling, and tidbits for praise and encouragement. Keep corrections to the absolute minimum. With a young puppy, ignore the incorrect or use a mild reproof such as "Ah-ah" or "No."

Choose places to train that are quiet and relatively free of distractions. This is important initially when your puppy is young, and its ability to concentrate is limited. Later on other locations and distractions become a part of training. Work with your puppy for only a few minutes at a time. Five minutes or less is enough time. Try to do this several times during the day. Always end on a good note.

It is difficult for a small puppy to relate to an adult whose voice seems to come out of the sky. It is rather like relating to a skyscraper! Children usually establish a good rapport with a puppy by their natural tendency to get down to the puppy and put their faces next to its. A spontaneous and immediate relationship develops. Adults, somewhat inhibited along these lines, tend to pick up and cuddle the pup—nice but not training. A puppy should not be picked up too much, but encouraged to stand on its own feet with its person coming down to its level. A person towering over and staring down at a puppy is intimidating to it.

All puppies are afraid of the unusual: sights, sounds, and places. It is a perfectly normal and natural reaction. *How* the pup acts is critical. A poised puppy initially reacts in fear, then recovers, is sensibly cautious, becomes curious, and wants to investigate. How you respond is even more critical, since the pup takes its cues from its leader. Your attitude and approach affect the puppy's reactions. If you have a calm, matter-of-fact style, while encouraging the pup to investigate, you will develop a self-assured dog. If you overreact, so will your dog in time. For example, some people who want a "brave" dog encourage excess aggression. When the aggression is combined with fear, often a dog develops the response of biting when afraid. On the other hand, if you coddle your dog, supporting its fear, you are teaching it to be fearful and insecure. Sensitivity, part of the dog's natural behavior, enables it to discriminate among situations and to react appropriately. Don't discourage it.

Dogs are sensitive to noise. If gradually conditioned to different noises from puppyhood, the dog learns to accept them as part of the natural scene. These noises include normal home sounds, traffic, motors, pounding, as well as loud, shrill, sudden, or continual sounds. Country dogs often find the city overwhelming, but the city dog, raised on noise, has no problem with the countryside.

You want your puppy to be adaptable, able to get along well with other people and dogs, to be at ease in different places.

There are, however, limits to the amount of public exposure that a young puppy should have before it has had its vaccinations (see Chapter 9). After that it can visit with friends, make the acquaintance of their dogs, and walk in the neighborhood of its home. Gradually, it can be taken to different places, inside and out. Most people you encounter are kind and will be interested in spending a few minutes talking to and petting a new puppy. Dogs are great conversation starters.

It is important for the pup to accept new hands on it, but it should only have to contend with one or two people at a time. It will grow weary, and you must know when to stop the attention. As the pup learns to accept new individuals, it can move to the larger scene easily. Crowds are difficult, with masses of large bodies rushing about and bumping into or stepping on the pup: hold the lead short to keep the pup close for security and protection. Although the situation is exhausting and should be brief, the puppy gains confidence and assurance with each trip.

A dog should be able to meet new people easily. Although its attitude should be friendly, the kind of overtures it makes depends on its basic personality. Some dogs approach readily—

eager for attention. Others are diffident or reserved, approaching cautiously. Do not force the issue. Most dogs are afraid of some people, as the result of actions that seem threatening to them. In addition, dogs take their behavioral clues from their leaders' reactions. When you are in a comfortable situation with friends, you respond very differently than you do in an uncomfortable situation or with someone whom you dislike, distrust, or fear. There are subtle scent changes that make your dog acutely aware of your feelings and enable it to size up people and make correct responses. Respect your dog's reactions. Canine appraisal is very accurate!

The pup should also learn to get along with other dogs. This includes having them in its home as well as being a guest in theirs. The well-behaved canine is at least reasonably friendly with other dogs. They may or may not play with each other, but neither puts on a display of dominance or defense. That is unacceptable behavior. Assume that your dog will behave, thus projecting confidence to the dog, which *tends* to live up to your expectations. A watchful eye and a readiness to correct are also needed, however. Canine size makes a difference too; little dogs often feel intimidated by larger ones.

First Words. The first word that any dog should learn is its name. The name should be a one- or two-syllable word with some zip to the sound, good carrying quality, and appropriateness for the particular dog. If the word is said in an eager, expectant tone, the puppy soon learns to identify with it and looks up and wags its tail when it hears the word. To teach the name, say it a couple of times, encourage the response with praise, and repeat it again several hours later. When it is repeated endlessly, the puppy tires and learns to ignore it, thus learning to disobey. Once the puppy has learned its name, it should be said in different tones of voice to see the effects on the puppy. This experiment is done to educate you, and a single brief session should be sufficient.

The other word all puppies need to learn is the corrective,

WATCH. The dog's attention is focused on her person. She is ready to learn. Signals by hand and foot are good ways of teaching the dog to pay attention.

"Ah-ah" or "No." The puppy must learn to associate this word with its action and to stop whatever it is doing immediately. There must be a sharp enough edge to the voice to convey immediacy and disapproval to the dog, never a hesitant or questioning tone.

Paying Attention. Because sensory information is such an important means of learning about the world, dogs are continually alert for new sensations. In terms of training, this means that dogs, and especially young puppies, are easily distracted. Once the puppy knows its name and "No," it should begin to learn to pay attention to you and to look to you for leadership. The easiest way to teach this is to get down to the puppy's level and to encourage the pup to look at you by talking to it and petting it or giving an occasional tidbit. Gradually, a command to look up is introduced. I like WATCH,* but "'Tention" (from "Pay attention") is an equivalent. Choose one and stick with it. When the word is said and the puppy looks up, it is rewarded with praise. If the puppy jumps up, it can be gently discouraged with "No" in a low voice to keep it under control. This lesson, lasting but a few seconds, should be repeated a couple of times a day.

The command to watch is used throughout the dog's life to demand that the dog put its attention on you and on the job at hand. In time, it will learn to watch and ignore whatever else is going on. That is too much to ask of a young puppy, however.

Backsliding. No learning has ever proceeded smoothly! It goes by fits and starts, largely dependent on the learner's emotional state at the time. It is easy to be distracted, lose concentration, forget, or not feel like learning. Human learners do that; so do dogs.

The young puppy is an agreeable sort and as long as the task is fun, it goes along, happily accepting praise. Sooner or later that stops. One day, that obedient pup will look at you defiantly or uncomprehendingly and proceed to do nothing or just the opposite of what you want. Your response is crucial. You must be in control and you must act quickly. The best step is to back up to an earlier point in training, to something the pup knows and can easily do and for which it can be praised. If the pup is clearly in no mood for training, doing a small, successful dab and then quitting is the best solution. You have stopped on a good note, the pup was taught the discipline of proper response to command, its feelings were respected, and you have retained the leadership role. Puppies must not be

*Basic commands are set in SMALL CAPITAL letters throughout to facilitate reference to them.

allowed to establish this into a pattern in which they call the tune, however.

It is a good idea to examine the reason for the backsliding. Perhaps you progressed too fast; the pup was confused, tired, or distracted; or you were inconsistent. Another factor to take into consideration is age. Puppies go through one or two independent stages, at four to five months and at sexual maturity. At these times—when the pup has grown physically and knows a lot but lacks much sense—it rebels against leadership. These testing times are normal but can be difficult. As long as you remain firmly in control, the pup learns to accept the relative roles and settles in happily. Heavy-handed tactics are not necessary for the majority of dogs that receive good early training.

The treatment for backsliding is to accept that it will happen, find the cause, back up in training, and begin again. Dog training calls for flexibility, an imaginative approach, and plenty of patience!

One of the most important things the dog learns in its puppyhood is how to "read" your body language. That subject it really masters—learning about you and your moods far better than you might imagine. The dog also does a considerable amount of training of its own. Anyone who trains animals should be at least as good a student of behavior as the animals are.

7

Companionship Training: Home and Car

The basic education that your dog needs to become a good companion and to be acceptable in human society is companionship training. The training directions in this chapter and Chapter 8 are intended specifically for the person with a young puppy (seven to twelve weeks old), but with some modifications, they can also be used for older dogs.

Dog training has seldom been approached with understanding or compassion. Several years ago I was teaching a college class dealing with instinct and learning. A student described training hunting dogs: "You beat 'em till they do what you want." When confronted with criticism, he added defensively, "But that's all a dog can understand." The thinking he reflected is not that unusual.

The heavy-handed approach is traditional and prevalent. Many people believe that the dog must be "shown who's boss" and that the only way to do so is by the use of physical force. The dog, then, is conditioned by pain or discomfort to do, or not to do, certain things, thus learning through avoidance or fear. This approach had long been the accepted one for training large or aggressive dogs for hunting, guard, or military work. It was then continued by trainers who moved into the business of teaching obedience classes for pets of all sizes and temperaments. Most trainers, whatever their background, train by imposing their will on the dogs, that is, *impositional training*. Usually the trainer is sure of his methods and uses the psychological device of blaming the dog if desired results are not obtained. Thus by labeling the dog as stubborn or willful, justification is found for using harsh methods. This can produce a cycle of harsh punishment for unwanted behavior, bringing forth more undesirable behavior and still harsher treatment, until at last either the human or the dog gives up. The dog's personality can be forever altered by such training.

Those people who are uncomfortable with such tactics often go to the opposite extreme. They may condemn all training, want no restraints placed on their dogs, and allow them too much freedom, or they may simply ignore their dogs. None of these approaches is desirable. All dogs need an education for their own sake as well as that of their humans and the neighborhood.

There *are* other ways to train a dog than through force or indulgence. *Inducive training*, as explained here, is based on a knowledge of the dog, its natural behavior, and modes of communication and enables you to work with your dog to mold acceptable conduct.

Training methods vary with the temperament of the individual dog. Breed differences are less important than are basic behavior and the degree of dominance or submissiveness of the particular dog.

HOUSETRAINING

Teaching your puppy to be acceptable in your home means that it must learn its place in the family, what it is permitted to do, and how to be alone. The puppy learns house manners, self-control, and responsibility. Once your puppy has learned these lessons, it will be acceptable in all parts of your home, other people's houses, and public places. You will, in short, have a well-mannered dog.

The usual word is house*breaking*, a term with an unpleasant association that is not used here.

The properly housetrained dog can be left in the home, and it will not destroy anything. It spends its time dozing, chewing its toys, and looking out the window. No puppy is capable of that level of responsibility.

Before the new puppy arrives on the scene, arrangements for its care should be made. This planning includes who is going to be responsible for the pup as well as the facilities for it. Remember that the puppy is still a baby with a baby's inability to control itself. Housetraining is usually its first experience of being taught. It is important that the experience be positive to give it a good attitude for further training.

The Den. In the wild, all canids live in small caves or dens. Dogs like private little places where they can retire away from the bustle of life and seek these out in corners or under furniture. You should provide some sort of den for your dog.

Most people who have a number of dogs use crates for them; each dog has its own. The ordinary person regards these as cages and may recoil at the idea of using one. To the dog, though, it is its own private and secure little den. If you wish to use a crate, it can be purchased, borrowed, rented, or built.

The den is a real asset in housetraining a puppy when you do need some means of confining it. Do not, however, overdo its use.

No dog should spend its life viewing the world from the confines of a crate. Excessive confinement from puppyhood tends to restrict the dog psychologically, inhibiting its ability to deal normally with space. Such dogs are easily frightened—they are "spooky"—and often have trouble adjusting to ordinary living conditions.

The Toilet Is Outdoors. The toilet is not in the den, on the rug, along the corridors or in the lobby of apartment houses, hidden in dark basement recesses, or in the neighbor's garden. It is in an appropriate location outdoors.

Dogs are naturally clean and are creatures of habit. These basic facts are used to teach the puppy the proper place to excrete.

Beginnings are important. If the puppy was raised in a clean environment, where the papers were continually changed, dishes picked up, and all the puppies kept clean, it has a head start on training. It accepts cleanliness. On the other hand, if it lived in dirty conditions, these too, were simply accepted. Puppies follow their mother's lead, so a well-trained mother, who teaches her children by example, is a real asset in housetraining. The pups are apt to continue the patterns of their early ways.

However, it is always possible to unlearn old habits and acquire new ones. Like people, dogs are learners. Although learning new habits is obviously easier for younger animals, age is not a hindrance to learning. Do not accept dirty habits on the assumption that nothing can be done about them.

The directions given are for the use of a crate, but you can modify them for other arrangements.

First thing in the morning with the minimum attention to your own dressing and grooming, get the puppy outdoors. As you open the crate door, ask the puppy in an eager, but not excited, tone, "You want to go out?" Get it to the appointed place as quickly as possible. You may need to carry it, especially if some distance is involved. The apartment dweller, having made his dash, walks his pup, sees that it excretes, and gets it back inside with no difficulty. Not so the country person, who is apt to dump the pup in the yard and go indoors. Stay with the pup so you know where and when it excreted. Little pups, especially first thing in the morning, usually excrete several times. Do not be tempted to go in after one small puddle.

When the excretory activity has been taken care of, take the puppy inside and let it run around in a confined area under supervision. The kitchen is best. Keep an eye on the puppy, talk with it, and feed it while having breakfast. The puppy should learn to clean its dish within a few minutes. Don't allow the puppy to nibble, go off, and come back for another bite. That encourages fussiness. When the puppy leaves its dish, assume that it is finished, pick up the dish, and do not feed again until the next meal. It will quickly learn to eat promptly.

After eating, the puppy will continue to frisk about the kitchen. Watch closely. After a few minutes, often as few as five, the puppy's behavior again suggests that it needs to excrete. It becomes restless, or it circles and then squats. Puppies do that remarkably fast and often. When play behavior begins to change, again ask, "You want to go out?" or shorten it to "Out?" collect the pup, and get it outside. Return to the same spot previously used, unless it was, by accident, in a poor location. Try to select a good spot and return there on each outing. The location and the lingering scent help make the proper association for the dog.

After the second trip out in the morning, put the pup in its crate with a chewable toy. As you do so, use some words that it will learn to associate with the crate. I use DEN; others use "Bed," "Crate," or "Kennel." The word itself is not important, but whatever you choose, stick with it. In time the puppy will go in by itself on that word, just as it will respond to "Out?" by indicating its need to go outdoors by running back and forth, jumping up, or going to the door.

Once in the crate, the pup should settle down and sleep for several hours. If not, cover the crate with a towel or blanket to darken it while allowing air to circulate. Leave the puppy alone. When it wakes, out it goes again.

The training sequence, then, is outside to excrete, inside to play and eat, outside again, inside the crate to play quietly and to sleep. It must be repeated at regular intervals during the day.

* * *

During the period of most rapid growth, from weaning to five months, the puppy has to eat frequently—four to six meals a day are usually needed. As growth slows down, so does the appetite, and the number of meals can be reduced. People who are away at work all day have problems with such a feeding schedule, but it can be solved by leaving a dish of dry food or several large biscuits for the puppy to munch on during the day. The biscuits have the advantage of combining entertainment with nourishment.

If you are at home during the day the sequence is based on four-hour intervals. Set up a schedule so that you do not forget the times to take the puppy outside. It is easier on the pup than the situation in which no one is at home during the day. However, puppies are adaptable and learn to adjust their schedules to yours. If you leave home to go to work, the training sequence takes place before leaving, on returning, and twice during the evening.

If your job keeps you away longer than eight hours, and especially if it has an erratic schedule, I think it preferable to provide a small pen around the den. Put papers in one part for the puppy to use. The first person home should promptly attend to the dog's need to get out. Consideration demands nothing less. Think how often you have gone to a bathroom during that same time!

A young pup about three months old *can* go through the night without excreting provided it is confined to a crate and the house is quiet, but eight hours is about the longest it can wait. It learns to accept the routine and settles down in the crate easiest when tired. You can expect the pup to wake with the dawn and to cry; this is the time to get it outside promptly. Puppies develop this amount of control at different times—one should not expect it at two months, and it may well be after three. Consistency is very important in establishing the routine; the puppy cannot be expected to get up at 6:00 A.M. on weekdays and sleep until noon on weekends. As they get older, puppies are better able to wait and less urgent in their demands to go out. Older juveniles and adults often learn to adjust to considerable vagaries in the schedule.

The puppy's bladder and bowel controls are well developed by the time it is four months old. Its habits should also be. It has been my experience that the puppy left in a pen often learns to stay clean by that age and does not use the papers provided.

At the beginning of training, the puppy may excrete in its crate. It didn't know that was not the proper spot, or perhaps it was not finished before it had to come in. Make no comment, but clean it up *promptly,* using a deodorant cleanser. A common mistake at this point is to leave the pup in the crate with the mess on the assumption that it will not like this and will learn not to do it again. It does learn: to accept living in dirty conditions. This unintentional training is a drawback to your ultimate goal. If the accident occurred on the floor, do the same prompt and quiet cleanup. Have the puppy out of the way while you clean up.

Some of the indoor play time should be spent in training and some in just being together. Have the puppy on your lap or next to you while you read, watch television, write, or converse. Cuddle, stroke, and talk with it. Do not allow the pup on rugs or furniture alone. If it goes to sleep, let it stay as long as you wish, but if not, watch for restlessness.

One of the day's outings should be a walk for educational, as well as excretory, experience. In good weather, be outdoors with the puppy as much as you can. Use the time for exercise, play, training, or just being together. Enjoy the puppy! Don't park it in the yard and forget about it.

Sometimes time and weather conditions make you wish the dog would get about excretion promptly. A hurry-up command is a helpful addition to the dog's vocabulary. I use "Go pee" in an urgent tone; "Hurry" and "Be good" are more genteel equivalents.

Almost every puppy goes through a difficult stage when it

COMPANIONSHIP TRAINING: HOME AND CAR

seems determined to do what is not wanted. Perversely, it does not excrete. You have stood at the chosen spot in the pouring rain. You have walked. Nothing. Put the puppy back in its crate until the next regular outing. In this way, as with the removal of a dish of food, the puppy learns the consequences of its actions. It does not take many such experiences for the puppy to learn what it is to do and where.

Expect backsliding as a normal part of the learning process. Human babies do that, too. When your timing was good and you stayed outside long enough, and there still was an accident, do not get agitated. Scold briefly, clean up, and forget it. When backsliding takes place, back up in training. In this case, reduce the amount of free time, perhaps to the initial amount, and then gradually increase it again. This bolsters the learning and hence is preferable to nagging or harsh punishment.

The training program is a learning experience for you both. You are learning canine body language. It will take you a while to master that. Do not punish the puppy for your error in reading its signals. Watch closely and learn. Take the time to study the puppy's behavior even as you are modifying it. Training is not a matter of imposing your will, but of inducing the dog to do your bidding.

The type of training involved in teaching the puppy where to excrete is essentially positive. Correct behavior is established by routine and rewarded by praise; negative behavior is ignored or treated by a quick reprimand. Extremely harsh methods, employed by unknowing people, teach by intimidation, a technique that has other long-lasting and undesirable effects.

The training to be described in the remaining sections about housetraining is different from that used to teach the puppy where to excrete. Now you will essentially be training by correction: unwanted behavior is discouraged or prevented by reprimand or, where needed, by physical action. As always, consistency is necessary in order to make it clear to the pup that certain behaviors are not approved.

Exploring the House. The puppy should get more freedom as it develops and learns to control itself. Gradually extend the play time, and when it can be free in the kitchen for about thirty minutes safely, begin to let it explore other parts of the house, room by room, for a few minutes at a time. Stay with the pup.

Keep the exploration as pleasant and low-keyed as you can. Be on the floor with the puppy. Do not restrain it. Encourage exploring and encourage coming back to you. Praise when it does so by voice and petting, but do not pick up the puppy. Too much of that can teach overdependence or an unwillingness to come, as it does not want its activities interfered with. Neither is desirable.

Watch its behavior as it dashes into new territory and then gives everything in reach a detailed sniffing inspection. Interesting things are also tried for taste, exactly as the small child puts everything in his mouth.

Teach the puppy that sniffing is allowed but nibbling is not. As it begins to pick something up, give a mild reproof, "Ah-ah" or "No" in a low tone. The pup should look toward you and may even come. If it ignores the correction, repeat with more authority. As soon as it leaves the object, praise the pup even if it merely lost interest.

In order to avoid a constant barrage of correctives, remove some of the more obviously interesting objects and hazards, such as electric cords. Toss a familiar toy in the room.

Once you have been through the house room by room, start over. Don't remove as many items or even any of them. Encourage exploration but correct each time the pup starts to lick or mouth something it is not to chew. "Ah-ah" is quite mild and has the desired effect on some dogs but absolutely no effect on others. "No" is a stronger word and can be said with more assertion. Use the mildest correction that does get a response. Without responses there is no training.

There comes a time in the life of every puppy when it must seize the delicately turned leg of an end table in its mouth and settle down for a good, long chew. If you have been teaching and the pup learning, it is very likely to roll its eyes around at you to see your reaction. This is a testing time. You respond with a sharp "No," and the very instant the mouth parts company from the table's leg, you rejoice with praise. Do not be tempted to dart after the pup, which it will regard as a game, or to correct more severely.

But if, in spite of your reprimand, the puppy goes right on with its chewing, you know that it is demonstrating its independence and stronger measures are in order. Go to it. Do not sidle or sneak; walk with determination, giving the impression that you mean business. You do! Take hold of the scruff of the neck or the collar and give a short, sharp shake, saying "No" very firmly. No doubt it will squeal. Ignore this. Several such treatments may be necessary, but if you deliver them in the proper spirit, the chewing should stop. A strong-willed dog may require the still more extreme measure of cuffing it under the chin.

Notice the progressive level of correction. First a mild reproof, then a stronger one, then a shake, last a smack. It is important to use the progression. If you start out hitting the dog for anything and everything it does wrong, there is nowhere else for you to go for stronger measures. Furthermore, you have either taught the dog to be hand-shy or defiant, neither of which is desirable. Always use the mildest correction first, working up to something stronger if and when that does not work (see Chapter 5).

Table Manners. The well-mannered dog does not interfere with the family's meals or beg for food from the table. To teach that, always feed your dog before the family eats so it is not hungry. Generally, if you ignore the dog, it will simply settle down somewhere; you can enforce this by telling it DEN (or "Go to bed"). If the dog sits mournfully beside you, ignore it. If it jumps up, push it down with a curt OFF, giving a quiet, kind word in praise for compliance. You can also train your dog to lie down beside your chair with DOWN and STAY (see Chapter 8).

FRIENDSHIP: YOU AND YOUR DOG

Be sure you do enforce this and do not allow the dog to get up and wander about at will. That teaches the dog to ignore your commands.

Respect for Persons and Property. Left to its own devices, your dog will happily take over all of your home, making it into a colossal den, decorated according to its tastes. Dogs are possessive and like to carry off objects of interest, chew on them, and secrete them in private places for future reference. These canine tendencies may well be in conflict with your ideas of management and decor. Before the dog begins to take over, determine the standard of conduct that is acceptable to you. Set up the rules, teach them to your dog, and stick by them yourself.

Your dog wants to be with you and should be. That means that it can be in any part of your home without destroying anything of yours. You cannot expect this type of conduct from a puppy. Be reasonable. For example, do not expect your dog to stay out of the living room when you are at work all week but allow it to go into it on weekends. The dog cannot tell which day it is. But if you have to keep your dog out of certain rooms, or confined to others because of its destructive tendencies, you have not properly housetrained it.

The matter of dogs on furniture is a personal one. There is no question that the dog prefers to be on the nice, comfortable furniture if given its own choice. Limits must be taught. I have no objection to my dogs' lying quietly on furniture, but I don't want roughhousing there, and I also want to use the furniture. To teach them to depart, I use the command OFF, pointing to the floor and assisting them to get off. Some people say, "Down" or "Get down," but that is too much like the command to lie down and is confusing. If you do not want your dog on the furniture, don't let the puppy get up there in the first place. When it comes to you while you are sitting in a chair, stroke and talk with it quietly. As the forepaws come onto the edge of the chair preparatory to invasion, say "Off" firmly and push the paws off. Praise it when the pup is on the floor.

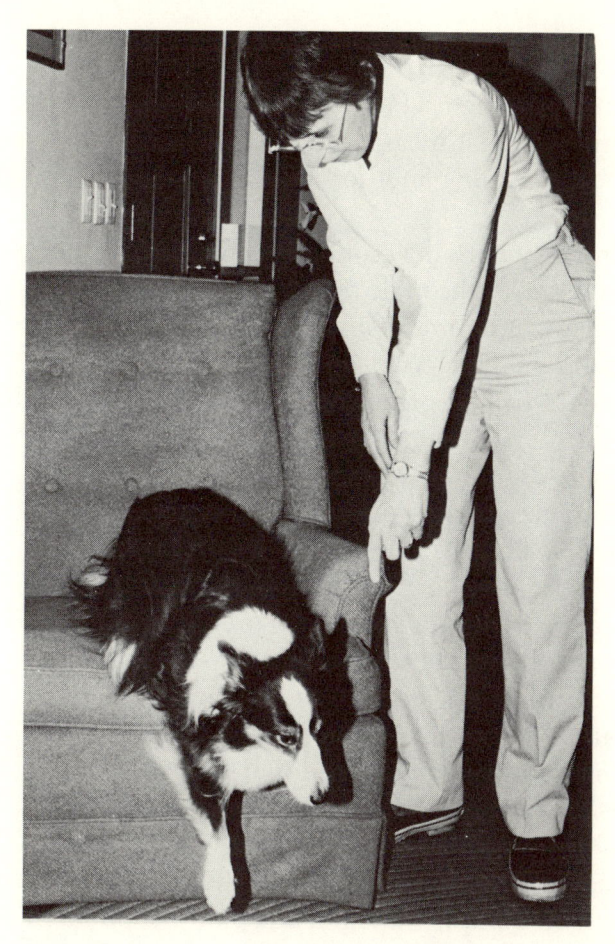

OFF. When directed by command and signal, this dog is quick to leave her chair.

You may not mind the dog's getting on some pieces of furniture, but really don't want it on that brocade heirloom. Fine. Repeat "No" whenever it makes an advance on that chair, never allow it to get up, and make no comment when it gets on other chairs. This requires consistency.

OFF is also used when the dog puts its face or feet on the dining table, the coffee table, the desk, or the counter. It is also used to stop the dog from jumping on people. This is taught by pushing it off firmly or lifting a knee to intercept a large dog while giving the command OFF. Praise is given when the dog is off even though you did all the work. You are teaching.

I prefer the word "Off" to "No" for these situations. "No" is an all-purpose corrective that means "stop it." It is too indefinite to be useful here, so using another word is helpful.

Respect for property pertains outdoors as well. Never permit your dog to run freely through the neighborhood. When walking it, do not allow it to excrete on the sidewalk or urinate on shrubbery or gardens. If an accident does occur, clean it up. Most property owners will be pleasantly surprised to see you do this.

Many dogs like to dig. They burrow their noses deep in the hole, reveling in the interesting scents, and they enjoy lying in the cool earth in hot weather. This is perfectly natural entertainment that bothers no one. You may, however, object to your garden's being dug up, and your neighbor surely will. In your garden, this is a form of copying behavior, but it is better not to present the opportunity by keeping the dog away from the garden unless you are there, too. Dogs that are confined outside for long hours alone become bored and may do a lot of digging. This type of frustration behavior is easily prevented.

Many puppies mouth people. Although this is a natural show of friendliness in a puppy, it is not acceptable conduct in an adult.

Discourage this from the start with a firm "No" every time the puppy takes your hand or a piece of clothing in its mouth. Praise as it lets go. In more determined cases, grab the muzzle and pry the mouth open while scolding. If that is not strong enough, pinch the lips against the teeth as you order the pup to let go. Use a strong corrective, such as "Stop it" or "Drop it." The verbal and physical discipline should make the puppy open its mouth. Praise it immediately.

Some owners object to their dog's licking them on the face; others do not. Consistency is important. If you do not wish it done, allow the puppy to show its affection in other ways, such as paw giving, hand licking, or nuzzling, or a special trick.

What is important is to recognize the dog's need to show affection.

Dog owners often do not object to their dog's jumping up as much as their nondoggy friends do, although the habit can be overdone and is hard on clothing. This is a show of friendliness on the dog's part. Decide whether or not you wish your dog to be allowed to do this and, if so, under what conditions. Some people do not allow their dogs to jump up, reasoning that the dog cannot recognize good clothes and so will jump up when it is not desired. I have not found that to be true. Possibly this is because, for me, being dressed up involves heels, stockings, and a skirt, manifestly different from pants. My dogs are taught not to jump when I am dressed up, but that it is all right to do so when I am wearing pants. As they cannot be expected to distinguish old jeans from a new pantsuit, I must arrange not to be greeted in good pants or must accept the jumping because it was my training procedure that allowed them to do it. If you do not want your dog to jump up on you, talk to your dog, pet it, and teach it the meaning of OFF. Keep your greetings low-key, not prolonged or effusive.

You must be able to take anything away from your dog. Here again "No" is too indefinite, so use another, stronger command such as "Drop it." Watch for any signs of aggressiveness manifested by snarling, growling, or biting. Talking is not aggressive, nor is smiling. In aggression the lips wrinkle and pull up, showing the teeth (they pull back in smiling). If there is aggression, stop it immediately with a quick smack under the chin, hard enough so that the dog gets the message. Usually only one such treatment is needed to teach the pup that you will not tolerate such conduct. Use this only for things that you do not want the dog to have. Do not torment your pup with a barrage of taking toys or food away; that merely teaches the dog to be defensive or insecure.

Stairs. Stairs can be a problem, especially those that are steep or angled. Canine vision is not very acute, making it difficult to see the end of the flight. Teach the pup on a short set of steps where visibility is good, such as those from a porch to the ground. Coax it to come to you and, if assistance is needed, put its feet on the steps. Do not use a lead. Pulling frightens a puppy by interfering with its judgment, and it is apt to resist and try to escape. In its clumsiness, the pup is likely to fall. Encourage its attempts, but do not be overly solicitous or risk injury by teaching it on too long a flight. It will take on greater lengths as it is able to do so.

Elevators. The puppy should learn to walk into an elevator, stand or sit quietly while it is in motion, and then step off. A relatively empty one is a help to begin training. The motion may bother a puppy, and a few matter-of-fact words or a pat are a help. Do not carry the dog unless the elevator is crowded and the dog small and likely to be trampled.

Alone in the House. Being alone for long hours is boring for the dog, and what it finds to do may not have your blessing. Do not give a youngster more freedom than it can handle. Never leave a puppy with a whole house at its disposal. Gradually build up the amount of free time under supervision, and it will be able to be loose in the kitchen while you are gone. Do not trust it with rugs and furniture until it has proved itself thoroughly in your presence and is well past the teething stage. In addition, give your dog a goodly bit of exercise before you leave it, to ensure rest. Leave something to chew on in your absence.

Puppy toys need not be purchased ones. Indeed, some of them are so flimsy that their squeakers readily come out and can be swallowed. The best purchased toys are hard rubber balls, rawhide chews, and solid bones (natural or synthetic). Ordinary household items do well, too: a piece of rope with knots in it, an old sock stuffed with crinkly paper, boxes, and cardboard tubes. There is some mess, but the pickup is minimal for the pleasure provided. Respect the puppy with its toys. Leave it alone or play with it. Don't tease.

Many dogs that are left alone become fussy and bark excessively. This is a very difficult habit to break; it is preferable not to let it get established in the first place.

Barking. You may want the dog to bark when someone comes to the house. You do not, however, want it to carry on over the least activity in the neighborhood. Teach discrimination. This is done by training the dog to stop barking on command. Allow the dog to bark in greeting, alerting you, or in warning. Learn to distinguish the tonal qualities of these different barks.

Most barking problems begin in the juvenile period, when the pup develops a strong sense of territory and the desire to protect it. This sense is very strong in some individuals and breeds and unless curbed can easily get out of hand.

QUIET, a strong, assertive command, is used when you want your dog to stop barking. To teach it, you must first get the puppy's attention, and that is not easy to do when it is barking. There are several approaches.

If the pup does not pay attention to you, try a counter-noise, slapping a rolled-up newspaper against your hand or shaking a can of pebbles. Once you have the pup's attention, command "Quiet." That is quite a trick to do while a delivery man is standing impatiently on the doorstep, saying, "Sign this, lady," and the pup is dancing around barking and trying to get out the door! Try to get a lead on the pup before you answer the door and also try to teach your dog to stay, rather than dart out the door, by using the command BACK (see Chapter 8).

Because the delivery situation is not one in which you can train the dog, you need to set up one where you can. Enlist a friend's help. That person comes to your door and knocks. You are waiting with your puppy on lead. Answer the door but concentrate on your training, not your visitor. Let the pup bark several times to alert you; then tell it "Quiet." Praise if it stops barking. Have your friend knock again; once again tell your dog "Quiet." Do this several times, always praising the pup when it obeys. Once it has learned a few other commands (see Chapter 8), begin to phase in SIT and STAY and BACK.

At other times, teach your puppy the command SPEAK. To do this, get the pup excited by making some interesting noises, then give the command with a lift to your voice and encourage it to bark to you. Praise when it does. Then begin to teach some control by stopping the barking with QUIET. By positioning the two actions together and by teaching the dog the commands for barking and not barking, you develop the control you need. Consistency is required.

CAR ETIQUETTE

The dog that can ride well enjoys accompanying its people on all sorts of adventures. Some training is usually needed to reach that point, though.

The dog should ride in the back of the car. It does not lean out the window, risking injury on sudden stops or flying particles in the eyes, and it does not interfere with the driver. Any attempt to jump from seat to seat must be discouraged at once with a firm "No" and sometimes by a helper who can drive while you teach the pup its place in the car.

Little puppies, still unsure of themselves or the car, can ride on the front seat next to you, where your presence and an occasional word are comforting. Car training, like housetraining, is an occasion when a crate is helpful. The close quarters of the crate make the puppy feel more secure. Be sure that it is level to prevent bouncing.

You want to associate pleasure with going in the car. Take the pup to places where it can get out and explore. Combine car training with socialization. Make it fun—not just going to the vet's for a shot.

Motion sickness is common. It is caused by apprehension, fear, exhaust fumes, and bouncing on rough roads. The first

This dog has good car manners. She looks to the person, obeying the hand signal, and will not get out of the car until told to do so.

sign of a queasy feeling is drooling. If it feels sick enough, the pup will vomit. Try to stop and get the pup out before that happens. Never scold or coddle a puppy for being sick. In most cases, motion sickness is emotional and temporary and is cured by riding. If that doesn't work, the pup has to be taught to ride. Sit in the stationary car with the pup next to you. Talk to it and let it explore. Once it is used to being in the car, start the motor without driving. After it is comfortable with the sound of the motor, drive a few feet (the length of a driveway) and stop. Gradually increase the distance. Try to stop before drooling starts and get the pup out to walk around, then settled in again before taking off. To facilitate training, go before a meal and provide adequate ventilation, a smooth road, and a short ride.

Although a crate makes a dog feel more secure, tying does not. It increases fear and frustration as well as the possibility of injury on an abrupt stop.

The well-mannered dog does not leap out of the door the minute it is opened but waits for the lead to be put on and a release word, like "Okay" or "Let's go" before leaving.

8

Companionship Training: Basic Obedience

Every dog needs some additional training to be a good companion. Building the bond of companionship between you and your dog is a slow process calling for a great deal of mutual patience, understanding, and affection. The reward is a truly deep relationship that will lead to years of enjoyment for both of you. Because of the bond-building aspects of training, begin teaching your puppy early in its life. The methods given here are appropriate to young animals. Be sure to train for only a few minutes at a time.

Most of these lessons are practical ones that teach your dog obedience to your commands, putting you in the leadership position with the necessary control over its actions. The last two, retrieving and jumping, are not the same sort of control commands. Fun for the puppy, they can form the beginning stages of teaching other useful and entertaining actions that both of you will enjoy learning and doing together.

Use your imagination (and books on teaching tricks). Once you learn how to communicate and your pup learns how to learn, there is no end to the variety of things you can teach it.

Be sure to keep a light touch and spirit of fun in all puppy training.

COLLAR TRAINING

Use a buckle collar that is heavy enough for the size of the dog. When it is first put on, the pup scratches at this annoyance, but it forgets before long, especially if the collar is kept on. It should be too snug to be pulled off over the head, but loose enough to allow a couple of fingers between it and the neck. Generally, round collars are used for long-haired breeds and flat ones for shorthaired breeds.

LEAD TRAINING

Stage 1. The Dangle. Once the puppy is used to having something around its neck, tie a piece of cord to the collar. It should be long enough so that about a foot of line drags on the ground. At first the pup will step on it, pull its neck, and look tragic. Resist all urges to laugh at or comfort the puppy and allow it to solve the line-dragging problem by itself. Watch without comment. When the puppy has figured out how to walk around the line, praise it and take the line off.

Stage 2. The Lead. After the puppy learns to walk with the line dragging, attach a four- to six-foot cord or lightweight lead to the collar. Let the pup drag this for a bit; then pick up the end and guide it. Spend a few minutes doing this for several days.

Next, while following the pup on lead, simply stop. Usually the pup will come back to investigate. Praise it for coming but stand still. Let the pup explore around you within the span of the lead's length. Follow some more. Stop again. Crouch down to the pup's level, but do not move from your position when the puppy wants to. You are beginning to teach it that it must attend to your wishes.

The dangle lead on a 48-day-old puppy.

Once that notion starts to creep into its mind, begin teaching it to go where you want to. Carry the pup a short distance from the house. Put it down and encourage it to walk back. There is a natural reluctance to venture into unknown territory; therefore, walking home is easier than walking away. After several walks back to the familiar, over several days, start reversing the process. Walk away and then back. Gradually lengthen the walks as the puppy is able to do it.

Stage 3. Controlled Walking. Once it has learned to walk on lead, the puppy quickly takes over and darts in all directions to investigate this and that while the person tags along. Shepherding breeds are particularly adept at diving between human legs, and the more dominant pups may nip at ankles or pants. These are manifestations of the herding instinct, but not acceptable behavior; the puppy must learn to walk nicely on lead.

Controlled walking is walking together. The dog walks beside its person, one to two feet away, neither one pulling the other, and the dog not interfering with the person's progress. This is the proper control used in taking the dog for a walk.

This Sheltie puppy, 54 days old, is just learning to walk on lead. She doesn't do it very well, but she does demonstrate the herding instinct of her breed.

By 62 days, she walks nicely on a loosely held lead.

Teach a command for controlled walking and a release word to free the dog from control to allow it to excrete or to investigate something. I use "Nicely" (from "walk nicely") and "Okay." Teaching controlled walking varies with the temperament and size of the dog. Regular training equipment usually is needed at this point—a slip collar and training lead.

Slip collars are made of chrome chain or nylon fabric with rings at both ends. Put the chain or fabric through one ring and attach the lead to the other. Now put it on your left wrist so that the chain or fabric that goes through the sliding ring goes over the back of your wrist, with the rings on the thumb side of your wrist. Give a quick pop with the lead held in your right hand. Notice how the collar tightens and then immediately releases. Take the collar off, turn it over, and put it on your wrist the other way around so that the chain or fabric comes through the sliding ring on the underside of your wrist. Again give a quick pop with the lead. Notice that the collar tightens and is held snug without releasing.

It is important that the collar should fit and work properly. The collar should be about two to three inches longer than the circumference of the dog's neck, to provide enough slack for correct operation. If it is longer than that, it is impossible to get the desired quick pop on the collar. In choosing a collar, be sure that it has good-size rings that allow the chain or fabric to slide through easily. Loosely woven nylon collars do not tighten and release as easily as chain ones do and tend to tangle with long hair, especially when both are affected by static electricity. Examine the collar carefully and try it before buying it.

The correct use of the collar is a pop-release. The pop is translated as a sudden snugging of the collar that the dog learns to recognize as a correction. The release, or looseness of the collar, means correctness; the dog learns that, too. The tightening of the collar comes across the back of the dog's neck, not on its throat—another reason the collar must be put on correctly. When properly used, the pop-release is both discipline and praise with a clear-cut distinction between the two. With small, young, or trained dogs, collar correction is made by wrist and

THE SLIP COLLAR.

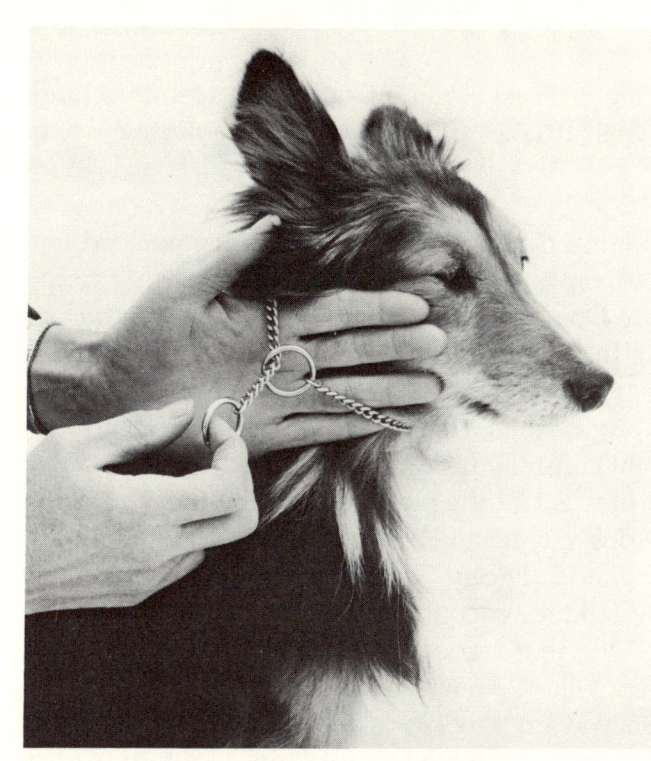

Correct position.

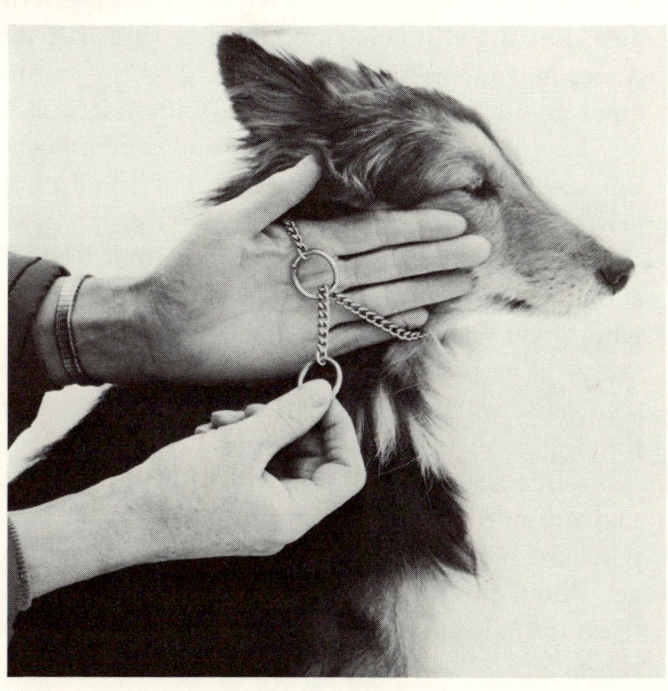

Incorrect position.

FRIENDSHIP: YOU AND YOUR DOG

forearm action alone; large or rambunctious ones require shoulder action, as well. It takes time to master the effective use of the collar.

A good training lead is substantial. It can be grasped and held firmly. The snap is secured to the fabric and will not spring open on its own. Do not use chain that is hard on the hands, or narrow cording that slides through too easily. Leather or webbing leads are the best.

If your puppy is small, sensitive, or a natural heeler, it can usually be taught controlled walking on a buckle collar, using a command and praise. Get the puppy's attention first by talking to it, using the dog's name and WATCH. Then, shorten the lead, repeat the name, add "Nicely," and step off. Continue to keep its attention by talking, encouraging, correcting by inflection: "Jack, Nicely. Oh, that's good. Stay with me now. Ah-ah, Nicely. That's the fellow. Awwwright. That's m'boy. Lookit that pup. Okay." Keep it brief.

This technique is not adequate for large, boisterous puppies. Put the slip collar on, making sure that it is positioned correctly. Get the pup's attention, give the command, make a quick pop-release with the lead, and start walking.

Keep talking, encouraging, and correcting as needed. In this case, the corrections are both vocal and physical. Still, be brief.

You must be consistent. You cannot train the puppy by allowing it to pull for a while and then hauling it in. Get it where you want it, encourage it to stay there by talking, and release it with "Okay." As you gain facility, alternate periods of controlled walking with freedom, both by command, so that the dog is always under control.

Discourage any nipping with a firm "No." If need be, grab the pup and shake, or slap under the chin. Repeat the "No" with the physical correction and praise when the puppy lets go. When the puppy bumbles into you, discourage that and teach it to give you some space by bumping into it if it gets too close.

COMPANIONSHIP TRAINING: BASIC OBEDIENCE

Stage 4. HEEL. In standard obedience training, HEEL is a command that tells the dog to assume and maintain a precise position at the person's left side. It keeps that position wherever the person goes and sits when the person stops. For the puppy, *heel* means within a few inches of the person, on the left side and on a loosely held lead. Do not attempt greater precision or the automatic sit with a young puppy.

Training the pup to walk at heel should be done with the slip collar. If it was not used to teach controlled walking, begin phasing in its use before the four- to five-month-old testing stage. It is a good idea to teach a puppy to heel because there are times when you need this degree of control. Get your pup's

HEEL. This is a well-trained adult. The hands are in good positions on the lead. The right one holds the excess, and the lead runs loosely through the left hand, which can tighten to make any needed corrections. The body is relaxed. Compare the handling here with the picture of poor handling in Chapter 5 (p. 63).

attention with its name, give the command HEEL, and step off on your left foot. Encourage the puppy by talking with it while you are walking and use little pop-releases for correction.

Practice both controlled walking and heel so the puppy learns to be versatile. Do not try to correct walking position errors by the use of "No," which is too indefinite to have any meaning at this point. Use encouragement and correction, verbal and physical means of teaching your pup. The pup should walk with you. Teach it to walk in a straight line as well as to weave, as through a crowd. Walk in circles or squares. Make right, left, about turns. Stroll, stride briskly, jog, run, go to different places. You are teaching controlled behavior; the puppy is learning that and the joy of being together. The bond of companionship is growing.

SIT

Anatomically, dogs are not built to be sitters. Because it is not a particularly comfortable position, they do not choose sitting for long, but it is a useful control position and easy to learn.

Get down on the floor next to your puppy. Steady the front end by putting your right hand on the collar or chest. Slide your left hand along the puppy's back, around its rump, and down onto the back of the rear legs. Keep your hand flat and the touch light. When your hand is on the top of the rump, apply a little pressure with it, hesitate slightly as you say "Sit," bring your hand around the rump, and tuck the legs into a sit. Do not push down on the back. Praise when the puppy is sitting. After a few times, the puppy will begin to get the idea, as evidenced by a slight bend or sag to the legs when you say "Sit." Encourage and praise at this point, but keep it low-keyed or the pup will forget what it is doing. As a variation, have the puppy facing you, and run both hands along the sides of the body. As they slide onto the hind legs, say "Sit," and ease the pup into the sit. Praise.

Another way to teach the SIT command is to hold a tidbit in your hand just over its head. The puppy looks up and often

SIT. The right hand steadies the dog while the left one runs along the back, around the rump, tucking the legs into a sit. The puppy is 62 days old.

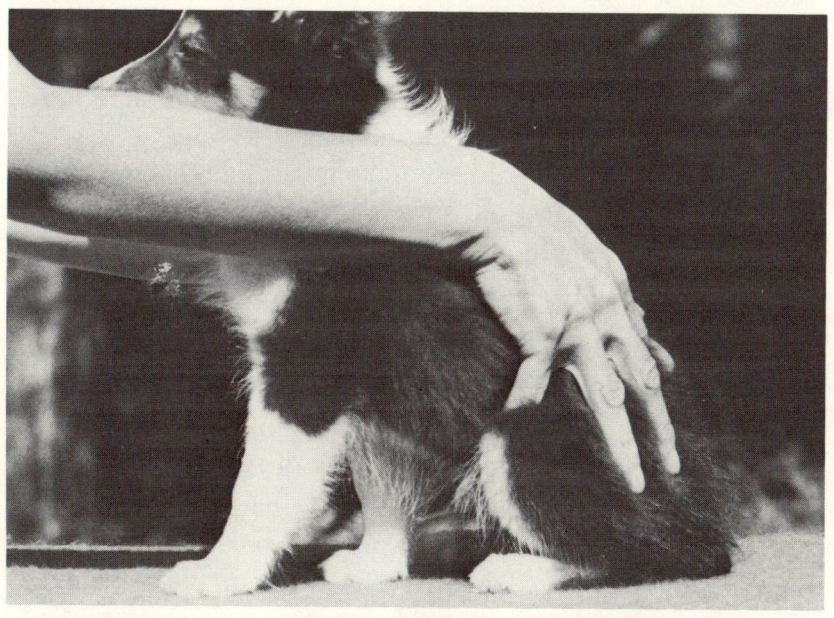

SIT. Another method of teaching the sit by running the hands along the sides of the body and easing the 62-day-old puppy into position.

backs into a sit. If not, it will jump up. Praise the sit and ignore the jumping or use a mild reproof.

Do not expect the puppy to remain sitting. That requires a different command. Praise for trying, then accomplishing, the actual sit.

Once learned, the sit can be practiced at odd times and in getting the pup under control for other activities, such as having the collar and lead put on, or focusing its attention on training before starting something else.

COME

Without doubt, the most basic training of all is to have the dog come when it is called. The dog must leave whatever it is doing and come promptly to you. It should always *want* to come. The goal is to teach absolute reliability combined with desire.

Unintentional training often takes place here. If you call your puppy and then discipline it, usually as part of housetraining, it associates the correction with the act of coming, not with the mess on the floor. It may then hesitate to come at another time, especially if it "reads" impatience or annoyance in your body language or tone of voice. Where discipline is required, go and get the pup; do not call it to you.

Start teaching your puppy to come as soon as you get it. Teach it that its greatest pleasure is to be with you by showing how happy you are whenever it is near. Do this by talking with and petting the pup. *Always* praise the puppy when it comes to you.

I use two verbal commands. COME is an authoritative word, implying urgency. The contraction "C'mon" is softer and less demanding and has fewer tonal variations. In one brief session, experiment with these variations to see the effect on your pup when either word is said happily or crossly, with your voice going up or down. Then practice putting your voice where you want it as the occasion demands. The inflection means as much as, or more than, the actual word, so voice control is important.

Stage 1. Beginning. Start this training indoors, where conditions are more controlled. Join your puppy on the floor. Let it explore for a bit; then hold out your arms in a welcome and call the puppy to you. Use its name only. Keep your voice light, happy, and expectant. Do not command. Make interesting sounds that attract its attention: clapping your hands, patting your leg, clucking, whistling. Encourage the puppy from its first tentative step in your direction all the way in. Smile. Tell it how good it is and pet it gently on the face, head, and back. Don't ruffle the fur, rub, or pound vigorously. Watch its reactions to see what gives it the most pleasure and use that information for later rewards. Most dogs do not like to be grabbed at; many do not like rough handling. Respect these feelings.

As the puppy learns its name and makes the proper association, it will look up and wag its tail when it hears its name. Don't overdo its use. Begin to phase in "C'mon" in the same gay tone. Do this several times a day, but no more than two or three times at a session. Increase the distance until the puppy will come bounding to you from anywhere in the room.

Stage 2. Short-Line COME. Begin the short-line come as soon as the puppy is lead-trained, using the four- to six-foot lightweight lead. While walking the pup, stop occasionally, crouch down to the puppy's level, and call it to you. Keep your voice happy and arms open. Next, back up a few steps, call, and guide the pup in with the lead. Work up to standing erect. Always praise enthusiastically as soon as the puppy starts to move toward you. The puppy should be responding to its name, enticing sounds, the verbal command "C'mon," and a signal (outstretched arms).

Begin to teach COME. Give that command in a firm tone after using the name. The pup should be somewhat startled, look up, and beat a hasty retreat to you. But if it does not, repeat the command coupled with a quick pop with the lead. You may well need the assistance of being on the puppy's level; drop to it quickly.

COME. The puppy, 48 days old, on a six-foot, lightweight lead comes happily to an enthusiastic, open-armed welcome.

COME. The body position is more erect. The signal to come is given with one hand while the other one helps guide the puppy, five months old, in with the lead.

108

Do more lead work, letting the puppy explore while you follow along. Once it is busy and paying no attention to you, sing out the name, followed by "Come," a quick pop on the lead, and praise all the way in. Back up sometimes to give more distance.

Once all of these variations are reliably done indoors, do them outside, before proceeding to the next step.

Stage 3. Long-Line COME. Attach a ten- to fifteen-foot cord to the buckle collar and take the puppy to a place where it can explore. Let it do so and forget all about you. Once it is out at the end of the line, call the puppy's name, followed immediately by "Come," a quick tug, and praise. When the puppy gets to you, let it bounce around to show its happiness while you praise copiously. I like enthusiasm, so I encourage my pups to jump up and then shower them with encouragement.

Next, repeat this, using the slip collar. You may need to start that quite early if the pup is big or headstrong. When you call, give a snap to the lead at the same time, thus emphasizing the command.

Ideally, you will not need to get down to your puppy or open your arms in welcome, but if the pup is at all hesitant, these familiar signals may be helpful and should be used quickly.

Work for reliability on the long line in different places and with distractions. If your puppy is now at the testing age, you may need a more solid jerk to get its attention and start it coming.

Introduce all sorts of variety in coming. A particularly good variation is to call your pup, then turn, and run away. This capitalizes on the chasing instinct, is fun, and makes the pup come quickly. Praise enthusiastically.

Stage 4. COME *and* SIT. By now, the puppy has also learned to sit. Use the short lead, call it with COME, and tell it to SIT when it arrives. Be prepared to put it into position. Reward both the coming and the sitting with praise. In time, the puppy can come and sit by itself.

Stage 5. Off-Lead COME. Once the puppy is reliable on lead and with distractions, you can begin to teach it to come without a lead. Start with the pup only two to four feet away from you, call its name to get attention, and follow immediately with COME. Have confidence in your pup and your training, but take the precaution of doing the first few off-lead calls indoors or in a fenced yard. Be especially careful about doing them at the stage when the puppy is testing its independence. Even well-trained pups can get smart-alecky then. When training, do most of your calling on lead, interspersing an occasional off-lead come among them. This means that your puppy will not know exactly what to expect and will pay more attention to you.

In the independent stage, a puppy may suddenly discover that it is off lead and decide not to come or to run away. Do not grab at it, chase, scream, or panic. Keep your temper, be calm, get the pup, and put the lead on. The most effective technique for getting the dog is casually to walk off in the opposite direction, virtually ignoring the pup. Curiosity takes over, and the puppy follows you. Praise it wholeheartedly when it catches up to you. Then do several short calls on lead with plenty of praise. Continue for about a week at the less advanced, on-lead level before trying it again off lead.

The rigor and expectation have increased in a regular progression with these exercises. Enjoyment and reliability should have also. The pup becomes proud of what it can do and of pleasing you; always show pleasure in return.

I use several means of summoning my dogs to me. They respond to their names, the familiar form of address used around the house. "C'mon" means "come along with me" or "check in" when they are running free. The emphatic "Come" means "get to me this instant." I also continue to use a signal to come: an arm held out or moving inward in a beckoning gesture. They also learn that in formal obedience training for competition, they are to become alert on their names, remain still until the COME command, and then come straight, quickly, and sit in front of me.

Response to a whistle is useful for dogs that can run free, because the sound carries better than the voice. The dog can be trained to a human or a purchased whistle. If you use your own, use the same sound consistently and make it of several notes.

The well-trained adult dog has no problem responding to all these variations. It takes time and maturity to reach that level. Don't expect it from a puppy.

STAY

STAY is a control command, which you can begin to teach after the puppy has learned to sit.

Tell the pup to SIT; then bring your hand, held flat with the fingers together, in front of the pup's face and say "Stay," pulling the sound out: "Staaay." The hand signal acts as a momentary deterrent to moving, and that is exactly how long it

STAY. The left hand, holding the puppy, acts as a deterrent to moving while the right one, directly in front of his face, gives the signal to stay. The raised hind leg is a sign of submission. The puppy is 74 days old.

should remain, a moment. Praise quietly. Repeat this two or three times. Crouch or kneel, beside or facing the pup, but do not move after telling it to stay. Work up to an erect stance.

Gradually lengthen the time to a few seconds. Raise one hand toward the puppy's face, at its eye level, and repeat "Staaay" only if it looks hesitant. This action teaches the verbal command, the signal, and paying attention.

Teach the puppy to remain sitting while you praise it with quiet words and gentle petting. You may need an extra "Stay" or signal to help. Then release it with "Okay."

Once the pup is able to sit and stay briefly while you are standing, work on getting a little distance between you. Sit the pup at your left side, give the STAY command and signal, step off on your right foot, and pivot around to face the puppy, toe to toe. Praise and release. Work on extending the time to several seconds.

You should also gradually extend the distance, but don't aim for more than six feet with a young puppy. Keep its attention on you by means of the hand signal. Don't talk. Stand in front, to one side, or behind the pup. Return and praise before letting it move.

When a dog is preparing to shift position from a sit to getting up or down, it extends its head and neck forward. At that time, say "Ah-ah" or "No" in a low voice, repeat "Stay," and hold out your hand at eye level. Never require a puppy to remain in position more than a few seconds; it is simply incapable of concentrating any longer. As it gains confidence from training and as it matures, the time can easily be extended to several minutes.

When it is steady on the stay, begin to combine this with coming. Have the puppy on lead, tell it "Sit," then "Stay"; step off on your right foot (another signal); walk to the end of the lead, turn, and face the puppy. Call its name and "Come." Lavish praise on it for its accomplishments. Teach it to wait for your directives by returning sometimes and calling it at other times.

SIT and STAY. Both the hand and the foot signal the stay command. The five-month-old puppy is watching closely.

DOWN

Although the natural resting position for canines is lying down, it is a more difficult position to teach than sitting. Being required to lie down is an act of submission. Older dogs, and especially dominant ones, resent having to assume the submissive posture, and teaching this can be a real leadership battle. Young puppies, still fairly submissive at least, are much easier to teach.

The dominant-submissive roles are minimized if you are on the pup's level. Sit on the floor with your legs folded. Have the puppy sit against your legs. Ease it into lying down by cradling its back against your legs, leaning forward, and gently extending the legs out as you say, "Down." Do not push down or pull the legs out. The position of your legs provides support and is also reassuring. Once it is down, praise quietly. Do not expect it to remain down. Practice this two or three times at a session.

DOWN. Step 1. The puppy, 62 days old, sits against the leg, which gives him some support.

DOWN. Step 2. Cradled against the leg, the puppy is eased down.

114

DOWN and STAY. Step 1. This 5-month-old puppy knows both commands and is learning to put them together. The hand loosely resting on her shoulder is a reminder to stay.

DOWN and STAY. Step 2. The hand is lifted slightly but ready to go back if needed.

As a variation, have the pup sitting facing you while you kneel, holding a tidbit in your hand at eye level; then slowly lower your hand to the floor in front of the pup and move it back. Most puppies follow this gesture and sink into a down position. *As* it begins to slide forward, say "Down," and praise when it gets there.

Once it has learned DOWN, begin to combine this with STAY. Start at the beginning of the training directions for STAY because the puppy cannot automatically transfer what it knows about sit and stay to down and stay. Although it must be taught, the puppy usually makes the association more quickly than it did the first time. DOWN and STAY can also be combined with COME for additional variety.

SIT and STAY. Learning by mother's example, this attentive five-month-old puppy is also helped by the lead. His mother enjoys her role as teacher.

STAND

Standing is another control exercise that is often difficult to teach.

Sit on the floor beside your puppy or put it on a rubber mat on a table. The latter is preferable because the puppy is less sure of itself and more apt to pay attention to you. Run your left hand along the side of the body to the curved part of the hind leg and cup your hand around the curve to straighten it as you say "Stand." Another technique is to put your left forearm under the belly just ahead of the curve of the hind leg. Lift your arm, brushing the curve, and say "Stand"; then rest your arm lightly against the belly as you praise the puppy quietly.

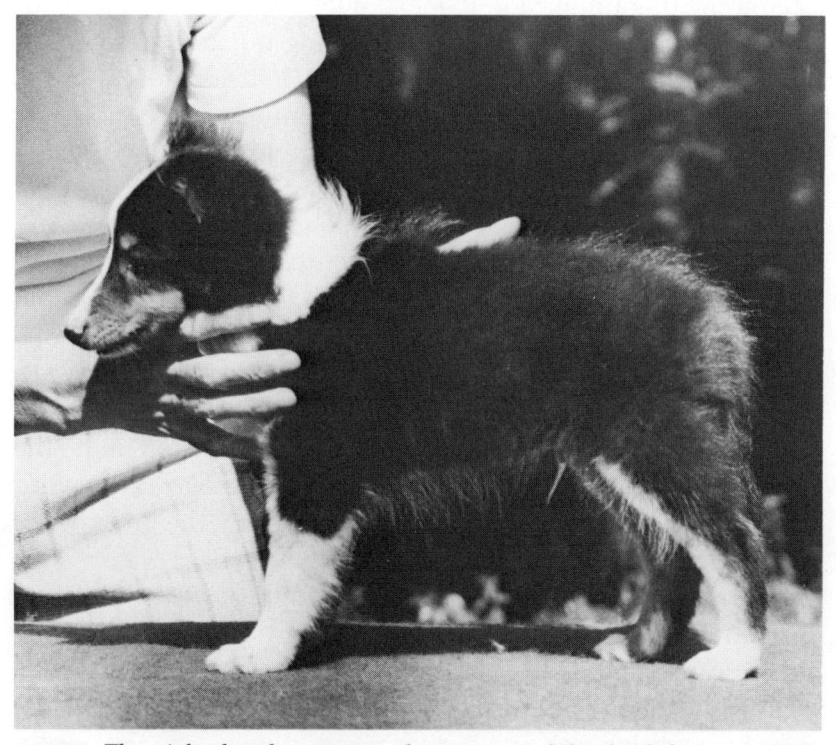

STAND. The right hand supports the puppy while the left one, which straightened the hind legs into a standing position, has moved to support the puppy's middle. He is 62 days old.

STAND should also be combined with STAY. Once again you will have to start with the initial directions for the stay.

The practical application of STAND and STAY is to steady the dog for grooming and examination. Combine grooming with training as soon as the pup is able to do so, but keep the session brief. Do not expect the puppy to stand for more than a few seconds; if the grooming takes longer, release it for a break with "Okay," and then reposition it. Gradually it will be able to stand longer.

BACK

The BACK command is used to prevent a dog from going through an open door. It enables you to go in and out without having the dog underfoot, to let someone in, to get the dog out of the way, and to keep it from jumping out of the car.

Have the pup on a short lead at your left side, reach for the doorknob with your right hand, and command BACK. As you do so, swing your left hand, holding the lead, out and give a slight backward tug on it. Extend your left leg or foot in front of the pup, blocking its progress. As it hesitates or steps back, praise it. In time, it will learn to do this on its own.

In the car, put the puppy on a sit and stay while you attach the lead. Then release it from the stay; gather the lead in one hand, the door handle in the other; and tug back on the lead as you say "Back." Open the door and get out, blocking the exit with your body; repeat "Back," if necessary; and then invite the pup out with "C'mon" or "Okay." At this stage, keep your hands free for the dog—don't attempt to carry the groceries at the same time.

Gradually you can train your pup not to leave the house or car until you tell it that it is "Okay" to do so. But absolute steadiness to this, as to any command, is a matter of maturity as well as training. The puppy is only learning. You can be sure that if something enticing comes along, it will seize the opportunity to bolt out after it. Take proper precautions even while you are teaching the commands.

BACK. The well-trained dog steps back on command and does not try to go through the open door until directed.

FETCH

Teach your pup to retrieve not only for its usefulness but because it is fun and, incidentally, a good form of exercise.

Get down to the puppy's level with an interesting toy, such as a ball, a sock tied in a knot, or a piece of paper crumbled into a ball. Play with it a bit yourself, tossing it from hand to hand to attract attention. When the pup comes to see what you are doing, ask in an excited voice, "You want it?" Toss it up and let it land about a foot from the pup. Let it pounce and carry the thing off. Make some pouncing maneuvers of your own in an attempt to get it back. Retrieve and toss again. Play with the puppy and the toy. Use no commands.

Dogs have different retrieving abilities. Some immediately dash after an object and bring it right back for more. Others get it and carry it off to some private spot. Still others go to the toy and stand over it as if they are not quite sure what to do with it. Then there are those that are totally uninterested (see Appendix 2). Much of this is the result of selective breeding, but all puppies are curious and love to chase and play. Try to get your pup into the spirit by encouraging it to play. Be the playmate, not the dominant leader.

Dogs perceive and relate to movement. Be obvious about tossing the toy around. Hold one end of a sock against the floor and wag it back and forth. Roll a ball so that it hits a wall and rolls back. Don't get anything too far away from the pup, or it may lose track of it. Once the pup will go out and pick something up, encourage it to return to you. Repeat right away. Keep up the spirit of play, until the puppy seems to tire, so that it does not get the idea that bringing something to you stops the game.

When the puppy will go out, grab the toy, and come back with it more or less regularly, start teaching a command. I like FETCH for its sound and carrying qualities; others use "Get it" or "Take it." Simply begin to phase in the command as you toss the toy and encourage the going out and coming back with lots of enthusiasm. Keep the atmosphere and tone of voice full of excitement and pleasure. If the puppy begins to get rowdy, tone down your voice and use a calming word like "Easy." For those reluctant to release the object, teach GIVE. If it has already learned to relinquish something on your command, there is no problem with GIVE. Simply take hold with one hand, say "Give" firmly, and be ready to encourage any slackening of the jaw. Do not play tug games or pull the object from the puppy's mouth. If it refuses to let go, grab the muzzle with the other hand and press the lips firmly against the teeth while repeating GIVE. When it squirms and opens its mouth, praise.

FETCH. Retrieving can be taught easily by using a dirty sock. It is waved around to get the puppy interested and then tossed a couple of feet away. Here she picks it up . . .

. . . and is guided back by the lead. She is 62 days old.

A good way to wind up a training session is with retrieving. You are still training, of course, but to the puppy it is a game.

JUMP

Another enjoyable and exercising activity is jumping. Most dogs like to jump, although some are better at it than others because of their physical structure. Jumping must be taught properly in order to make it pleasurable and to avoid subsequent problems.

Always provide good footing. Takeoff and landing surfaces must have some give to them; the best are grass, dirt, or carpet. Avoid slippery floors, concrete, and asphalt. Use only low barriers, two or four inches high, because you are teaching a command and how to jump, not vaulting. This is particularly important for puppies of large and especially heavy-boned breeds, which do not develop good coordination as early as the little fellows do. However, the structure is still developing in any puppy and injury could result from straining.

I feel strongly that the lead should not be used initially to teach jumping to a puppy. It must learn its own timing, a matter of visual determination, decision making, and muscular coordination. The pup, not you, must determine when to take off. The lead interferes with its decisions. It is apt to look up at you, especially if the lead snugs, throwing its timing off. Looking at you can cause it to trip over or bump into the barrier. This is not the time for WATCH.

An easy way to teach jumping is to put a narrow board across a doorway (open the door and wedge one end of the board between the door and the wall). If the floor is not carpeted, put a runner under the board. Step over the board and encourage the puppy to come to you. Do this only two or three times and praise it well. If the pup does bump into the board, do not coddle it, but immediately have it go over once again to prevent any chance of its becoming afraid.

After the puppy jumps easily over the barrier, begin to phase in a command. I like JUMP for its snappy sound; "Over," "Hup," and "Up" are used by others.

Keep the jumping enjoyable and couple it with other exercises like coming and retrieving. Work outdoors, too, placing the board between two trees or providing supports for it. Always keep the barrier low until the pup is physically mature. Six to eight inches is the maximum height I would use for a

JUMP. The board is propped up across the gateway into the yard. The puppy, 74 days old, jumps easily in response to the command. In order to have him learn his own timing, the lead is not used to teach jumping.

puppy. Do not push the puppy to do this and respect any hesitancy. It may not yet be ready for jumping. If you are teaching jumping to a nearly-grown pup or to an adult, use a buckle collar and the lead to *guide* the dog over the barrier.

TRAINING THE OLDER DOG

The directions given for basic obedience training are aimed at the usual situation: a person starting with a young puppy seven to ten weeks old. However, people do acquire older dogs, too.

Often the older dog has problems. It may not have worked out in its former home for one reason or another, and the people wanted to get rid of it. Patience and skill are required to establish acceptable behavior in the new situation. Generally, those who are inexperienced with dogs are better off with a new puppy and proper raising from the start, because it is always easier to instill good habits than to correct bad ones. There are, of course, many cases in which later acquisition works out well for both the person and the dog.

The first task after acquiring the dog is to establish the bond. Puppies bond strongly to the person with whom they associate during the socialization period. After that time, they must break that bond and establish a new one. The dog must be at ease and have confidence in and respect for the new leader. That takes time.

Make the break a complete one. Do not let the dog have any contact with its former person until new bonds have been welded with you, but try to find out as much as possible about the dog's personality, habits, and training. Avoid going to the old home, where you will pick up the familiar scent on your clothes. Fall in step with the old routine. Use the same name and commands. Feed at the same time and the same diet, at least initially. Expect some upsets and accidents as a result of the change. Allow the dog to settle in to your home and routine before trying to effect any major changes.

Never force yourself on the dog. At best, it is merely friendly, reserving some of itself from you. Talk with the dog, walk it on lead, groom it, providing pleasure in the association. Respect its feelings and preferences. Give it time and space. If it wants to be left alone, do so.

Begin training. This is the best way to build the bond between you. Use the directions given for young puppies, shortcutting where previous training makes that possible, and enroll in a regular obedience-training class as soon as you can.

OBEDIENCE CLASSES

Training classes, a popular form of learning and entertainment for people and dogs, are found in all large cities and in many suburban communities. They provide a structured program in which the person is taught how to train the dog. The dog learns specific exercises and commands as well as how to behave in an acceptable manner with other dogs. The classes, canine social events, are fun for both people and dogs.

A group of dogs at an obedience class, all of whom have been told SIT and STAY. Their owners are standing opposite them. Beginners are on lead with the owners' holding their leads; leads have been dropped for more experienced dogs and removed for the most advanced ones.

Instructors and methods should be checked out before enrolling. The instructors are the most important part of the program. They need good background achieved through education and depth of experience; they must be knowledgeable about dogs and their training, as well as the way to work with people. Training methods must allow flexibility for individual dogs. The same techniques should not be used for a dominant or strong-willed dog as for a willing or sensitive one. No school should force all of its students into a common mold. A good measure of the approach used is the attitude of the students, human and canine.

Classes that are sponsored by established obedience clubs usually are better than informal ones given as part of park recreational programs. The instructors at the latter too often have done some training and showing with one dog and then applied for the job—really not sufficient background.

The members of obedience clubs tend to be interested in training for shows. Whether or not you wish to show your dog is not important, but that interest is reflected in the quality of training found in the classes.

Many classes do not accept dogs for training until they are about six months old; others provide special classes for young puppies (eight to twelve weeks old) where they can learn and socialize. These classes are taught by someone knowledgeable about puppy training who can also answer your questions about care. This is an ideal arrangement. Puppies should not be trained in a class with adult dogs until well into the juvenile period (about six months old), but their education should start long before that.

There is a great deal of expertise in canine matters available within the collective membership of a club, a handy source of assistance should problems arise. Advanced training, beyond the basic level described here and provided at classes, is both challenging and rewarding. So is showing.

9

Care and Facilities

One of the reasons for our long historical association is the ease of keeping a dog. A highly adaptable creature, at home in palace or shack, it desires only to be with its human, sharing completely in its human's life. It is content and loyal, never questioning the arrangements or provisions—sometimes suffering needlessly through our ignorance. As we know more about the dog's needs, we are better able to provide for its comfort, health, and safety, and by doing so, we increase not only the quality of its life, but of ours as well.

There are many good ways to raise and care for a dog. These need not be elaborate, but depend on your facilities, imagination, and knowledge, but mostly your concern.

NUTRITION

Basic Requirements. For any animal, food serves two essential roles: it provides the basic raw materials for building and maintaining the body, and it provides the energy to sustain life. All activity, including deriving energy from food, requires energy.

The food supply must be adequate to meet the animal's needs in both of these roles.

The basic constituents of foods are carbohydrates, fats, proteins, vitamins, minerals, and water.

Only carbohydrates, fats, and proteins are energy sources. Fats produce the most—nine kilocalories of energy per gram; whereas carbohydrates and proteins produce four kilocalories per gram. Carbohydrates and fats are inexpensive; proteins are not. Although carbohydrates (sugars and starches) are the principal sources of energy for human beings, the dog's need for them has not been established. They are, however, included in all commercial dog foods because the dog, also, can use them as sources of energy. Fats, another energy provider, are also used to make parts of cells, certain hormones, and insulation for the body. Proteins, however, are the most important dietary components. They serve mainly as building materials, rather than energy sources. Amino acids, which compose them, are the building blocks used to construct all of the major structures of cells, tissues, and in-between connective elements.

A large number of vitamins and minerals are also required for proper nutrition. The needed vitamins are A, B complex, D, E, and K. Unlike us, the dog can make vitamin C and therefore normally does not need it in the diet. Vitamins help regulate metabolic processes in cells, including both the formation of cellular components and the breakdown of food to derive energy. About fifteen minerals are also required; those needed in the largest amounts are calcium and phosphorus, for bone growth and maintenance, and potassium, sodium, and chloride necessary for a variety of cell activities, especially nerve and kidney functions. The other minerals, though vital, are required in very small amounts.

Water, although not a nutrient, acts as a solvent, diluter, and transporter of all other materials. That role is so important that life cannot long be sustained without water.

Adult dogs on maintenance diets require a minimum protein level of 20 percent, and any nonmaintenance situation requires more. Fats should be at least 10 percent of the diet.

Commercial Feeds. Legally, all commercial animal foods must have a guaranteed analysis and ingredients listed on the label, although that information is not very helpful to most people. The first three ingredients listed are those present in the largest amounts.

In a good-quality dog food, all of these are proteins, and often there are other proteins as well. Poorer-quality foods list proteins in only one or two of the first three ingredients.

Typically, both plant and animal proteins are used in dog foods. The usual sources of proteins are muscle meat, other edible portions ("meat by-products"), bone meal, eggs, cheese, milk, fish, whole grains, grain (wheat or corn) germ, and soybean meal.

Plant and animal tissues are made up of proteins containing the same amino acids. Although both can be used as protein sources, plant proteins contain some, not all, of the necessary amino acids, so that one or more of the first three ingredients listed on the label should always be animal protein. Most foods are a blend of several plant and animal proteins, thus ensuring that all amino acids are present in at least adequate amounts. Because meat is the most expensive protein source, it is not surprising that the greater the amount of meat, the more costly the food. The term *meat by-product* found on most labels is a catchall and rather a misnomer. It includes glands, such as liver, which are nutritious, as well as ground hooves, hair, feathers, and claws, which are not. Because all of these are protein, they technically fulfill the requirements for the guaranteed analysis, but there is considerable difference in the digestibility and nutritive value of various "by-products." Cheaper foods use more of them to meet the required quantity, if not quality, of protein.

A number of commercial foods also contain artificial flavorings (that is, "liver flavor"), rather than the product itself; these have taste appeal, not nutritive value. The additives are designed more to appeal to the buying public than to nourish the dog.

* * *

Dog foods are manufactured in three different forms: dry, canned, and semimoist.

The dry foods are made either as loose meal, in which the individual components are distinguishable, or as solid chunks, called *kibble*. The meal is usually moistened to produce a granular consistency for feeding. Kibbles are made by mixing the ingredients and cooking them to a gruel, which is further processed in one of three ways. It can be baked hard into biscuits. These are either broken into pieces for the basic ration or shaped like bones for treats. The second type of kibble, the expanded form, is the most popular type of dry food, found in all supermarkets. The gruel, mixed with air, is passed through a sprayer, which cooks it under pressure. It emerges from the nozzle as dry, puffy kibble. Some manufacturers spray the kibbles with fat to improve the flavor. The third type of kibble is the compressed form. This is neither baked nor expanded but dried and pressed into pellets. These foods are concentrated, usually the diets of specialists, and are available from dealers. Kibbles are fed dry or moistened.

The protein content of the dry foods is in the 20 to 30 percent range, and they yield fifteen hundred to eighteen hundred kilocalories of energy per pound of food. Many of these are superior foods and can be fed as the sole diet for the dog's entire life. They are easy to store and to feed.

Canned foods are either complete meals or meats. The complete diets supply 10 to 12 percent protein, five hundred kilocalories of energy per pound, and are about 75 percent water. The protein content is higher (40 to 45 percent) on a dry-weight basis; however, the dog must eat more of it to supply its needs. Canned meats, usually with "by-products," are mixed with dry foods for additional protein; they are not balanced and should not be fed as the sole diet.

Semimoist foods, comparatively new products, are packaged as soft chunks or hamburgerlike food. They have a higher water content than the dry foods and cannot be stored without some means of preservation. This is done by the addition of sugar, acids, or other chemicals as preserving agents. These foods supply about 20 to 22 percent protein and fourteen hundred kilocalories of energy per pound.

I prefer to feed my dogs one of the high-quality pelleted foods. This is a well-balanced, concentrated food, but it is economical because less of it is required to keep the dogs in good condition. In the past, I have used the best-quality expanded kibbles. My prime consideration in choosing a food is the company that makes it: I want a product made by a reputable company engaged in nutritional research and testing. The manufacturer can supply information about the ingredients used in its products and its testing procedures, as well as answering specific questions about feeding. This information can be obtained by writing to the company's customer services department at the address on the food container.

Individual Nutritional Needs. The basic nutritional requirements of the dog have been established by the National Research Council. Dog food manufacturers, well aware of these, formulate their products to meet, or exceed, the requirements. Those of different companies differ from one another in the particular ingredients used, especially the proteins, and in the form and digestibility of the food. Commercial foods that have met the National Research Council's standard are labeled "complete and balanced," though that may not reflect their nutritive quality.

The National Research Council's standard is inadequate. It is a single diet, applied to all dogs regardless of such obvious differences as age and amount of activity. It is, thus, a minimum standard, which in many cases is actually substandard. In an attempt to point up its inadequacies, some of the major dog food manufacturers formed the American Association of Feed Control Officials, which conducts feeding tests and which is responsible for the formulation of separate diets for dogs in different conditions.

Commercial foods made by the major dog food companies,

regardless of their form, exceed the National Research Council's standard for all nutrients and provide them in a form that the dog can digest. That is not true, however, of the "generic dog foods," many of which barely meet the standard. Nutritional studies are now being conducted on puppies raised on several different generic foods, and the results indicate nutritional deficiencies, such as slower rate of development and reduced weight gain when compared to puppies raised on standard brands. Other findings are improper bone development, anemia, skin conditions, weakness, and lethargy. Not surprisingly, such puppies have a greater likelihood of contracting diseases.

As a result of the various studies, the National Research Council is currently revising its nutritional standards for dogs.

Canine nutritional requirements vary considerably. Such factors as size, age, activity, stress, health, and breed all affect what is needed. Very active dogs, engaged in working or hunting, for example, need a great deal more energy than do less active house dogs. Tiny dogs have higher energy requirements than giants. They have a greater heat loss from the body, require more energy to maintain temperature, and may have higher metabolic rates, yet their tiny stomachs hold little, and they have the problem of getting enough food to satisfy their needs.

Stress situations, such as pregnancy, nursing, sickness, outdoor living in cold weather, rigorous work, training, racing, or showing, greatly increase the needs for energy and often for protein as well.

Growth and development impose great nutritional demands. Growing bodies need twice as much protein, energy, vitamins, and minerals as do those merely maintaining themselves. The highest vitamin-mineral requirements are for calcium, phosphorus, and vitamin D for bone growth. Many manufacturers provide for a puppy's different needs with specially formulated puppy diets.

The best food to feed is the one that maintains the dog in the best condition on the smallest amount of food. Good condition is a body covered with firm muscle, neither fat nor having its bones protruding; the skin not flaky or dry; the coat sleek and gleaming. The dog has a sparkle in its eyes and in its behavior—it glows with health and the joy of life. An indication that the food is being well digested is the production of a few small, dark stools each day. The amounts recommended on the package may or may not be the proper quantity to keep a particular dog in good condition, though. Feeding is always a matter of satisfying the varying needs of an individual, and adjustments in quantity or product may be necessary to achieve that.

Many people feed adult dogs once a day. I do not care for that practice and prefer to feed two smaller, equal-size meals morning and evening. In this way, there is always some food in the stomach, but never a large amount, and the dog is content. Ideally, dogs should be fed on a regular schedule, although that is not always possible for you to accomplish. They can adjust to variable feeding times with less discomfort, I think, if they are fed twice a day. Dogs should be avid eaters, diving in and cleaning up the food quickly. As soon as the dog finishes eating, remove the dish even if there are leftovers. Provide a separate dish for each dog and a bowl full of clean, cool water at all times and keep the dishes and utensils clean.

Myths About Feeding. There are several myths about feeding that can create subsequent problems for the dog. All-meat diets, which have been promoted in advertising, are not good because of their lack of balance. It is true that canids are meat eaters but not as we define the word: to us, *meat* means "muscle." Wild canids eat all parts of their prey, including the internal organs and the contents of the digestive tract; that provides the needed balance. But the dog does not live off kills and cannot be nourished by muscle meat alone. Among other problems, the amount of calcium and phosphorus is out of balance, frequently resulting in bone and kidney problems.

Some show fanciers, particularly those with large breeds, feed puppies larger amounts of food than are needed in the hope that they will grow into big, strong animals and do so quickly. Development, however, is a gradual process, and this practice often leads to faulty bone and muscle development. Oversupplementation with vitamins, minerals, or proteins is a form of overfeeding. Some vitamins are toxic in large amounts, and others are merely excreted when in excess. Additional protein is often provided not only for growth and development in pups but also as an energy source. Although it can be used for energy, it is not preferable to carbohydrates or fats and is more expensive. Supplementation is not necessary with a good-quality food and can be harmful. Use supplements only upon recommendation of your veterinarian.

Dogs enjoy "people food," and most of us gladly share it with them. Treats can be given for special and not-so-special occasions. Do not overdo it, though, or you will provide more food than necessary and disturb the nutritional balance. Treats should not be more than about 10 percent of the diet.

EXERCISE

To many owners, *exercise* is a euphemism for excretion, and once that has been accomplished, it is assumed that the dog has been "exercised." Dogs can become lazier than their people. For good health, both require daily physical exercise; the kind and amount depend on individual needs and activity levels. Generally, dogs can use a great deal more than they get. We, of course, are always limited by time.

You do need to make some plans for exercising your dog. Ideally, the exercise should involve moving at all speeds (walking, trotting, running) because different muscles are used at each speed, and thus all are kept in condition. Some of the ways in which dogs are exercised are discussed next.

Running Free. The simplest and oldest way of exercising the dog is simply to put it outdoors and let it fend for itself. It may well get exercised as it runs with others, chases cars and people, eats garbage, excretes in other people's yards, and makes a general nuisance of itself! The dog has no shelter in inclement weather and usually has but a brief and none-too-happy life. Such dogs are hardly satisfactory members of the household, much less companions.

Increasingly, communities rebel at wandering dogs and their messes and impose restrictions on their freedom. Cities, almost universally, have leashing laws; some also require a person to pick up a dog's droppings and dispose of them properly.

Tethered. Many people tie a dog up on some sort of tether. Usually, this is a makeshift arrangement with a chain that is, inevitably, too heavy or short. When properly set up, a wire guy line is stretched tightly between two uprights, well above your head and stretching for some distance. A ring or pulley travels along the guy line with a lightweight flexible line running to the dog's collar. That line should be long enough to allow the dog to move about freely and to lie down, without being so long that it gets snarled up in various impediments.

Walked on Lead. Walking them on lead is the way city people habitually exercise their dogs. Adequately exercising a large dog requires miles of daily walking—a task few are even willing to contemplate. As well as the distance involved, it is difficult for a person to walk fast enough to provide real exercise, at a trot or run, for the dog. Little dogs, which require much less exercise, have a definite advantage in this respect.

Some people exercise their dogs while jogging or bicycling. This is a good form of exercise but does require training for the dog, coordination for the person, and proper physical condition for both.

Yards. People who are seriously involved with dogs as well as many single-dog owners have fenced enclosures. Whether small pens or large yards, these permit the dog to move about freely while providing security.

FRIENDSHIP: YOU AND YOUR DOG

Supervised Freedom. A daily free run is wonderful if you live where this is possible. Your dog *must* have some training before that and must respond promptly to COME (see Chapter 8), or you will find that you have inadvertently created problems for yourself.

Training. Training is an excellent form of exercise. The dog that has been taught to retrieve will bring thrown toys back and can thus be exercised even in a small apartment. It can also be taught to jump low barriers—another small-space exerciser. Some communities allow greater liberties for the obedient dog, such as being able to run off lead in parks, under your supervision.

Play. Play is another good form of exercise. Once you know something about canine communication (see Chapter 3) you can learn to play with your dog in its way. The bow is the canine invitation to play. Watch your dog, then imitate it, and respond to its signals. The games you play together are of your own invention, ones that you both enjoy. Learn also to recognize your dog's vocal communicators (whining, sneezing, and so on), copy them, and gradually develop a play communication of your own. Children are particularly good at this; adults can learn.

In playing with your dog, it is important that the dog recognize your leadership. The dog will not set the limits; you must do so and see to it that the dog shows restraint and stops the game when you wish to. Don't let this become too rough.

Dogs also play with toys on their own. This can be encouraged, and it will continue longer in the dog's life than it would otherwise. The best toy for the companion dog is a companion of its own. Two dogs are hardly more work than one and keep one another company; many dogs, too, are happy in the company of other animals, such as cats.

The psychology of the dog should be considered in any sort of exercising arrangements. When running free, the dog is independent and assumes its place in the dominance order of the local pack. Even though the dog may spend a fair number of hours at home, there really is no human bond with this dog. The dog's freedom is its human's irresponsibility. Respect for the dog and for the rights of other people cannot permit this. When leashed to its human the dog is bonded both physically and psychologically. The human's dominance position is apparent to the dog because where it goes and when are dependent on the person's desires, not its own. The lead can prevent having encounters with other dogs, examining tantalizing odors, or bounding across the street. Yet, if it respects its leader, the dog readily accepts this limitation and even feels secure in such an undemanding relationship. On the other hand, tethering the dog is not the same thing at all. Here the dog is inhibited from going where it wishes, but the human element is missing and the dog is vulnerable. Some people enjoy teasing a tied animal, making its life a torment. Other dogs invade its territory, and it can do nothing about the threat but become frustrated; it may even be attacked by strays. Personality changes often take place, especially when the dog is virtually relegated to a life chained up in the backyard. Fenced-in yards give the dog a sense of security.

Yards and tethers are convenient ways to put the dog out to excrete, but not necessarily to exercise. Put the dog out while you are at home but don't go off and leave the dog alone outside for long periods of time. Notice that the dog put out to "exercise" frequently does nothing after excreting. It stands and waits, or sits and waits, or curls up and sleeps and waits. It does not exercise. It waits for you.

When a dog is left without human companionship for a long time, it becomes bored and the boredom may result in frustration barking (a community nuisance), digging, chewing, stool eating, or apathy, depending on personality. For the dog, its greatest feeling of security comes from being with its own person.

FACILITIES

Outdoor Facilities. The best outdoor facility for dogs is a fenced yard that provides enough room for them to run about. Before erecting any fencing, it is a good idea to see what others have and to discuss construction details with them. The type of fencing needed is correlated with the habits of the particular breed or individual dog. Some have a great tendency to jump, climb, or dig, and the fencing must be high enough and deep enough in the ground to prevent escape. Others respect boundaries and stay inside even low fences. Breeders can give considerable advice on the subject. All too many of them, however, merely create an enclosure surrounding a dog.

A view of my yard. Woven material on the fence cuts down on visibility, and the dark objects on the ground, which prevent erosion on a slope, break up the area into several terraces and provide something to jump over. Assorted objects for entertainment can also be seen: a tire, a low platform, and a high platform. The yard is surrounded by plants.

A yard should provide entertainment, not mere confinement. The doghouse complex in mine is to the right of the previous view. The house has an attached "carport" and benches on either side. The dogs enjoy all these levels, and the gangplank, from an old workbench to the carport, is a favorite. In the summer, the grapevine on the arbor above the doghouse makes a cool glade for the dogs (and provides grapes).

A yard is part of one's property. Planting around the dog's yard makes it less conspicuous, reduces visibility, muffles sound, secures the fence's bottom to the ground, and provides some shade. The plant life should be tough, nonpoisonous, and nonvaluable. Trees or bushes within the yard are also attractive. Plants need protection from dogs while they are young and are getting established.

Dogs are not particularly interested in mere space so it is a good idea to break up the interior of the yard with assorted devices for entertainment. A south-facing shelter is a protection against the weather. Its roof or a platform makes a good place for sunning—a favorite activity. Dogs enjoy assorted objects to get into, onto, run around, or crawl through as well as things to play with such as boxes, branches, bones, or more conventional toys. Once they have served their purpose and are no longer used, discard and replace them with new and different ones. Use your imagination.

The yard should be open enough that the sun reaches all of it during the course of the day. Sunlight is an excellent disinfectant and deodorant. One of the best tools of preventive medicine is cleanliness, so it is important that feces be picked up promptly and thus never accumulate. Long-handled tools are available for this purpose.

Ground cover is of lesser importance than sanitation. The easiest is whatever is already present, although grass may be killed and some soils are not very desirable. Good drainage is important, and sand or gravel is often used as a cover to

The crate and covered foam bed are convenient and commonly used beds for dogs.

An indoor puppy pen. The puppies, 62 days old, use only a small area covered with newspapers for their toilet. Their bed is out of the picture at the lower left corner. The box and rag are some of their toys.

improve that. Dirt, if not attractive, is natural; has some give to it; and can be kept neat by frequent cleanup and raking.

Indoor Facilities. Your dog will happily share all of your home, taking over the bed, the couch, the easy chair. If you don't want this, you need to establish the proper conduct from the beginning (see Chapter 7) and to provide suitable quarters.

Dogs prefer something enclosed, like the caves their wild kin live in. This is why crates (see Chapter 7) are so popular with dog owners. There are alternatives. A dog bed, whether homemade or commercial, can be an attractive addition to the house, although dogs, not caring about the style, are as happy with a rug or pallet in an out-of-the-way corner. All dogs are fond of padded circular cushions (like beanbag chairs).

A puppy should never be given the run of the house until it knows how to behave in it. Leave it in a crate or pen with toys while you are away (see Chapter 7). If you need to confine a dog to one room, use an expandable baby gate across the doorway; however, first check to make sure it cannot get its head caught in the open sections of the gate.

WEATHER CARE

Temperature extremes create problems for dogs. Just being aware of them can help you take the right precautions to make your dog's life safer and more comfortable.

Winter. Most dogs enjoy winter. Snow holds innumerable interesting odors. It is fun to bound through. If the dog lives in a heated home, however, it can easily become chilled by prolonged exposure to cold: it should not be put out and left unobserved. As long as the dog is active there is no danger, but once it becomes tired it stands or sits and hypothermia begins to develop. The dog shivers, lifts its paws alternately, and looks pathetic. Unwell, old, and young dogs are particularly susceptible to hypothermia; they can die of it.

If your dog is outdoors for any length of time, a good shelter out of the wind is a necessity, as is liquid water. Smooth-coated and particularly little dogs living in extremely cold climates may need a coat for added warmth over the chest. Generally, there is a greater need for energy in cold weather, and the ration should be increased, especially for dogs that are working outdoors.

Frozen bodies of water are real hazards. If a dog falls through the ice, shock and panic quickly set in, the dog becomes exhausted in its struggle to escape and all too often does not succeed.

Dogs walking on snow pack it into balls between the toes, where it freezes into icy pellets. The dog works diligently at nibbling them out. It should *not* be allowed to do so if it has been walking on sidewalks that were treated with melting chemicals, as these can be toxic. The snow balls should be worked out by hand, towel, and washing; they may also be prevented by the use of boots.

House dogs should not be left in parked cars in extremely cold weather. Once the motor has been turned off, the car begins to cool quickly, and the dog cannot move around enough to keep warm.

Summer. Hot weather poses even greater problems in the opposite direction. Most dogs do not enjoy heat to the same extent as cold, probably because of their origin as northern animals (see Chapter 11). Panting is not a very efficient cooling method, either.

Feeding and exercise should take place during the cooler hours, and the dog should be allowed to pursue its own amount of activity, or lack of it, during the heat of the day. Many dogs enjoy swimming. Lying on a sunny beach is not a canine preference, and the dog should not be forced to do so. Let it be near you, but in the shade.

Insects are annoying by their buzzing and biting, particularly about the face. A small amount of repellent applied on the back of the head and ears is helpful.

Shade is necessary for the dog whenever it is outside. Have plenty of fresh, cool water available all the time.

Summer is the season that requires the greatest amount of grooming: removing shedding hair and checking for inhabitants, rashes, bites, and burrs.

Car problems are also greater in the summer. A dog left in a closed car begins to overheat quickly. If the windows are wide open, it can still become too hot for the dog, but even worse is the situation in which the windows are barely cracked, for fear that the dog will escape or be stolen. If the dog must be left in the car in hot weather, the car must be parked in the shade with as much ventilation as possible, water provided, and the dog checked on frequently. The moving shade pattern can suddenly put the car in unrelieved sunshine. Overheating can quickly prove fatal.

GROOMING

Essentially, grooming is a matter of keeping an animal clean and inspecting the body. It is a lengthy and involved process for heavy-coated show dogs, requiring considerable expertise, but you can cope adequately with your dog yourself. When you groom your dog, you become more aware of its body and what

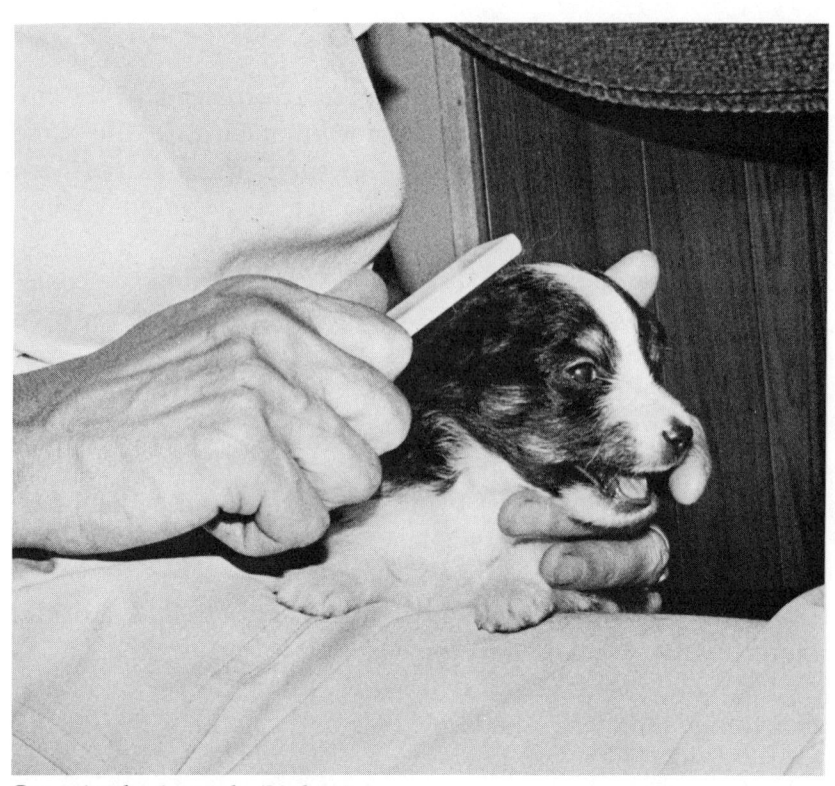

Grooming begins early (21 days).

gives it pleasure, thus building additional bonds between the two of you.

Dogs that have been properly taught will stand or lie quietly to be groomed, enjoying the process and the attention. A young puppy will not. It is important to teach it unhurriedly (see Chapter 8) and to establish the grooming routine as a pleasant experience. A pup should not be expected to stand for long and it should not be frightened. Professional groomers and breeders use special tables with nonskid surfaces for greater ease in working on the animals. Still, the pup needs time to get used to being on the table before any grooming is done. Once it is reasonably comfortable, stand the puppy up, stroke it, and talk to it in a calm, matter-of-fact voice. From stroking, you can easily move to brushing. At first, the brushing is as gentle as the hand; only later as the dog gains confidence does it become more rigorous. Dogs whose grooming style requires the use of electric clippers need to become used to the sound before any actual clipping begins. The puppy also has to learn to accept having its feet picked up and examined, its tail lifted, its eyes, ears, mouth, anus, and reproductive structures examined. Dogs that do not allow grooming have not been trained or have had unpleasant associations with it.

You do not need to invest in a grooming table; work on the floor or put a rubber-backed mat on a table.

Grooming should be done on a regular basis. Set up a simple routine. For instance, brush your dog gently all over to put it in the proper mood, then inspect it, and cope with whatever needs attention. Follow with a full and rigorous brushing accompanied by admiring remarks. Dogs preen themselves on admiration.

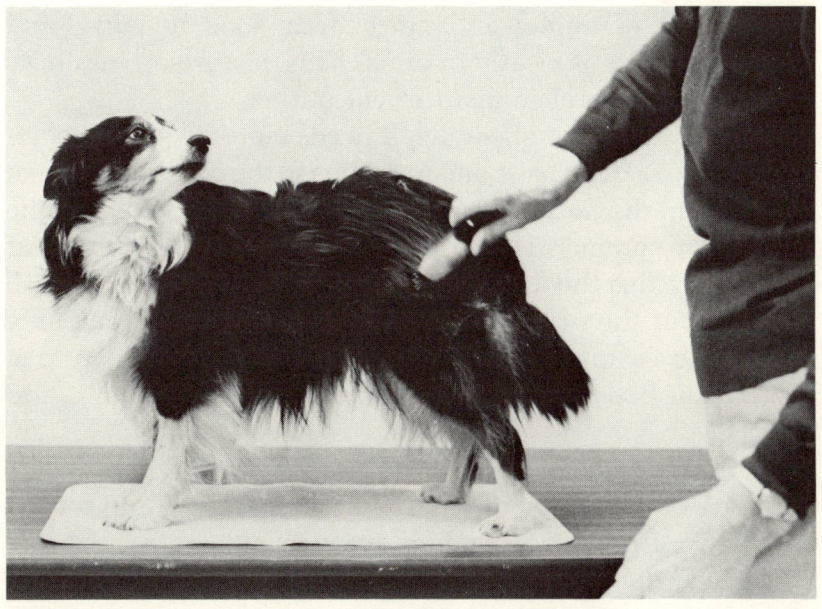

Brushing is enjoyable, and the rubber bath mat gives her good footing on a slippery surface.

The coat is the most obvious part of the body involved in grooming. It should be carefully brushed down to the skin. Some types of long coats are combed; others are not, or only where the coat is soft and apt to mat. Many long coats are damp-brushed to enhance growth and prevent breaking or pulling out the fur. Others are plucked to remove dead hairs. Trimming is often done to make coats neater. These details need to be discussed with someone knowledgeable about the particular breed. Professional groomers are also available to take over more elaborate care. All dogs, however, whether show dogs or beloved companions, need regular care to be comfortable and attractive. There is a lustrous sheen to the coat of a healthy dog in good condition. If it is dull or dry, adding some fat to the diet may be helpful, but if the dull, dry skin goes with a dull, lethargic dog, there are other problems and medical advice should be obtained.

Many long-haired breeds have soft hair that tangles easily on and behind the ears. Hanging ears with long hair can collect all manners of unpleasant things, from food to burrs, and regular combing is clearly in order. Tangles develop into mats that have to be broken apart or cut out.

When the coat is shedding, it needs more frequent grooming to remove dead hairs and to minimize the numbers of them flying about the house. Dogs should not be clipped all over the body in the summer. This thoughtless practice grows out of our assumption that the dog, like ourselves, would be hot under all that fur. But the dog does not have sweat glands all over the body. It loses undercoat in hot weather, and the outer coat protects the body against solar radiation, possible burning, and insects.

Care of the feet is important. Since they come into contact with all sorts of surfaces and are apt to be injured, regular care is needed. The claws should be short enough so that they just clear the floor when the dog is standing. Clippers are readily available. The blood vessels appear at the base of white claws as a pink area; cut just beyond that. Black claws are more difficult. If both colors are present, the black ones are cut the same length as the white ones; otherwise just remove the tip. Filing smooths any rough edges and shortens the claw a bit more. In long-haired dogs, hair grows between the toes and over the pads. Trim this hair short so that the dog walks on its pads, not a furry covering (there are exceptions for some show dogs). Long hair on the feet collects snow, burrs, gravel, and so on, and is slippery to walk on. Caught between the toes, these materials are painful and cause the dog to walk on the back of the large pad. The toes can spread apart and the foot become lame in time.

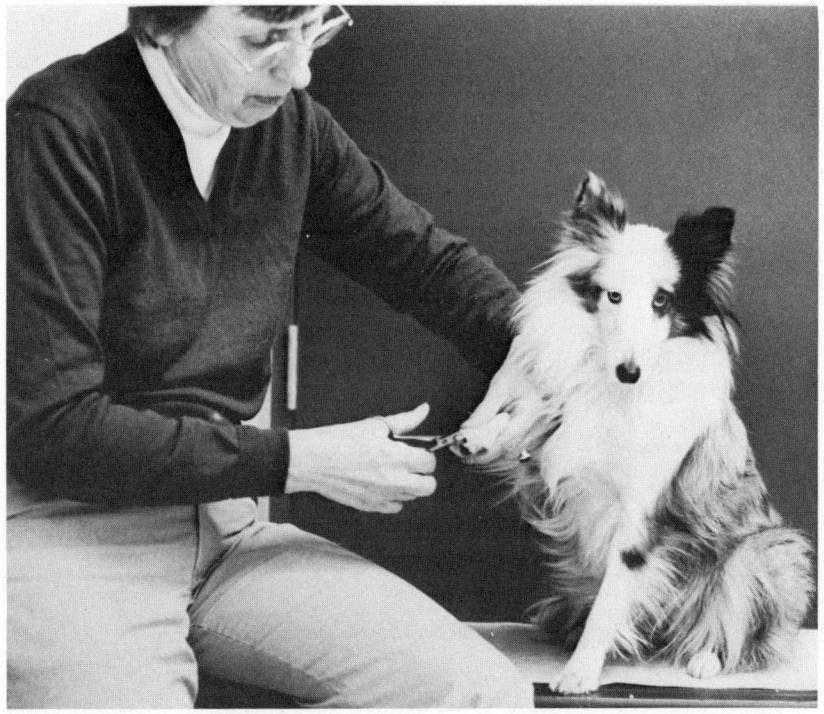

Clipping the claws is not so pleasant but is tolerated. Sitting beside the dog often provides a feeling of security.

Body openings also need regular inspection. The eyes should be clear; thick matter exuding from them requires immediate medical attention. The ear canal should be clean. It is not so well ventilated in dogs with hanging ears as in those with erect ears and is more subject to collecting secretions and dirt. Uncomfortable and unpleasant situations result and require veterinary attention. The ear mechanism is delicate and easily damaged by instruments or liquids; thus cleaning, hair removal, and treatment of ear canal problems are not jobs for the amateur.

The mouth is also inspected. The gums should be bright, not pale pink. The teeth should be white and smooth, but tartar accumulates, making them yellowish and rough. There is less tartar when hard foods are fed, but if the diet is soft, hard biscuits, bones (natural or synthetic), or rawhide chews can be given periodically to help clean the teeth. Natural bones should be solid and large enough so the dog cannot break them. Tartar is removed with a scaler by someone who knows how to use it.

The anus should be clean, not irritated or inflamed. If feces are of the proper consistency, they are deposited cleanly. Occasionally they may be loose, clinging in the coat. Wash it out and watch the diet for the next few meals. Too much of the highly concentrated foods can cause looseness. If looseness persists, consult your veterinarian. Penis, testes, and vulva should also be checked to be sure they are healthy.

Such inspections take only a few minutes and are helpful in spotting potential problems early. While it is being groomed, the dog has a sense of well-being and security at the gentle touch of its human's hand upon its body. Should more involved procedures—even painful ones—be necessary, the dog that is at ease in the grooming situation will accept these too in the proper spirit.

PREVENTIVE MEDICINE

General. Medical problems are facts of life for all living things. We should not deny ourselves the company of dogs because of

CARE AND FACILITIES

possible sickness or death, but we must do all we can to prevent disease or accident and then be able to deal with them when they do come. Awareness of the dog's habits and normal behavior can alert you to potential problems early, when treatment is easier and less costly. It is a good idea to cultivate an awareness of any subtle changes. A calm, matter-of-fact approach is the best one to take with a sick or injured dog, providing comfort and security while helping prevent panic. Frequently, an upset person will upset his dog far more than the sickness or injury itself! This is an additional stress for the dog to combat. The best tools of preventive medicine are good diet, exercise, cleanliness of the dog and its environment, and periodic health checkups and vaccinations. All of these go a long way toward preventing medical problems from developing.

The very best situation for any dog is to live with a sensitive and responsible human who has selected and is in communication with a competent veterinarian possessed of the same humane qualities. A good rapport is of utmost importance.

Inoculations. A very important part of preventive medicine is vaccination. Puppies receive their mother's immunity with their first milk (the first twenty-four hours after birth), but this gradually wears off and they are then susceptible to infectious diseases. The most common diseases are distemper, hepatitis, leptospirosis, parainfluenza, and parvovirus. They are covered by a common vaccine, administered in several inoculations on a definite schedule to young pups. Because the diseases are all widespread and often airborne, there is no way to guard against them other than vaccination. The dog then builds up its own immunity to the diseases so that when it does encounter the disease-causing organisms, as it surely will, its immune system will be able to combat them.

Most veterinarians advise annual booster shots to ensure that immunity levels remain high. This is particularly important for animals that travel or are under stress and for breeding females. Inoculation against rabies is required as part of licensing by many communities. As a result, the number of cases of rabies in domestic (but not wild) animals has declined in recent years. To help curtail the spread of this frightening disease, all animals with symptoms of rabies must be destroyed.

As well as receiving booster inoculations, breeding females should be checked for intestinal parasites because these can infect puppies before birth. Such puppies have an unnecessarily poor start in life. Questions about the mother's medical care are valid ones to ask a breeder when seeking a companion dog. The healthiest puppies are those produced by females that have received high-quality care (medical and nutritional) since their own puppyhoods. This is one of the reasons that well-raised pups are quite expensive.

One health problem is disease caused by the mass production and marketing of puppies. The pups are shipped and mingled with others at about the same time their natural immunity is wearing off. Mass producers are often casual about inoculations. Grouping puppies from a variety of backgrounds, under stress from being shipped, is a marvelous way for any sort of disease to be transmitted.

Most disease-causing organisms are specific for a particular animal, and thus canine diseases are not spread to humans, nor does the dog catch human diseases. The most notable exception is rabies, to which all mammals are susceptible.

Parasites. Parasites within and upon the body are part of the natural life of a wild canid, but they need not be for the dog. Preventing infestations is largely a matter of hygiene.

There are a number of external parasites that afflict the dog, of which fleas and ticks are the most common. Few dogs get through life without them.

When fleas are present, grooming reveals clusters of tiny pellets on the skin ("flea dirt") and the little flat creatures scurrying across the belly. A dog can be treated by washing with a flea soap or by using sprays or powders regularly. Flea collars can help prevent reinfestation. Fleas spend most of their lives off the dog, jumping back on for a meal; thus general cleanliness and the use of household sprays in the dog's environment are helpful in keeping down the population. A heavy infestation is uncomfortable, and the flea, the alternate host for the tapeworm, provides the source of another parasite. In order to lay eggs, female fleas must have a meal of blood, so any tactics that prevent them from doing so can break their cycle. Regular use of flea killers is necessary to keep them from getting reestablished, and they are very persistent. Some people have tried altering the dog's diet to make it less palatable to the flea, but the effectiveness is questionable, and you are better off sticking with the older methods.

Ticks, common in some parts of the country, are more difficult to kill. They burrow into the skin to feed and if pulled off are apt to break, leaving the head embedded, or to tear the skin. Put a little grease or oil on them, blocking the breathing apparatus; they then suffocate and drop off the dog. Dips, sprays, and collars are somewhat less effective for ticks than they are for fleas.

Worms are the most common internal parasite. Most of them live in the intestine, sharing the dog's food. When there is a heavy infestation, worms, looking like wriggling white threads, are passed in the feces. An advantage of watching the dog defecate or picking up feces promptly is that worms can be seen while still active. However, if only a small population is present, they may not be passed or observed.

Many people routinely worm dogs. This is a poor practice because you do not know whether your dog is infested—and if so, by what sort of worm. Different types of worms require different treatments. In order to be certain, a microscopic fecal examination must be done. Periodic examination of feces is good preventive medicine that reveals not only worms but other sorts of inhabitants as well.

Heartworm infestation is a growing problem. For many years, the disease was limited to the southern part of the country but in recent years has spread to most of it. Part of the life of the young heartworm is spent in the mosquito. When the mosquito bites a dog, it deposits some of these larvae into the bloodstream, where they develop. Adult worms live in the right side of the heart; in severe cases, the number of worms can block the chambers, valves, and pulmonary arteries, restricting blood flow and causing the dog's death. Treatment is difficult but prevention is not. Dogs in heartworm areas have a blood sample checked in the spring. If worms are not present, the dog takes medicine daily, which prevents the larvae from developing. Medication is stopped in the winter in areas of killing frost, at a date determined for local conditions by the doctor, but is continued all year in warm or tropical climates.

10

Fulfillment

The relationship between a person and a dog should be one that is mutually beneficial. Although the dog has been emphasized throughout this book, it is also appropriate to examine the human side of the relationship, to see what our needs are and how the dog can help fulfill them.

HUMAN NEEDS

Most of the requirements for sustaining human life are not unique to humankind but are also shared with other animals: food, water, oxygen, space, shelter, warmth, and companionship. We are primarily social creatures, associating together for comfort, security, assurance, competition, continually interacting and interdependent. Individuals nowadays belong to collections of small societies: family, community, ethnic, religious, professional, social, and so on, that compose the national society. Within the societies each of us belongs to, we learn our roles and how to interact with other members of the group. Cultural differences are readily apparent, yet underlying the differences are common threads showing that we tend to act in certain definite, and even predictable, ways reflecting our common human heritage. We are complicated creatures, highly intelligent, capable of great wisdom and compassion on the one hand, and great irrationality and cruelty on the other. We are motivated not only by intellect, but also by inner drives, emotions, and feelings.

Our social needs tend to reflect the way we feel about ourselves. We identify with the groups we belong to; we are supported by the group, and that support becomes a measure of our own self-esteem. The group's goals become our own. Acceptance by the group is so important that if a person is accepted and later rejected, he feels dejected and often devastated and worthless. Even when a person voluntarily leaves a bad situation and feels relieved to be out of it, he may still experience a sense of loss at the same time. Usually he seeks fulfillment elsewhere promptly.

Merely being with others is not sufficient to satisfy social needs. We must interact with them. Our communication system, the means by which information is shared, bonds individuals together in the social group. Body language, a holdover from a distant preverbal past, remains the major communicator of emotion and mood, but communication of ideas is by speech. We are compulsive talkers. Yet even as we speak, we are aware that words are inadequate to express particularly deep feelings. Physical expressions, particularly those involving the sense of touch—a pat on the back, holding hands, hugging—provide more comfort and assurance than words alone can convey (see Chapter 3).

The need for companionship is fulfilled in different ways by associating with other people of either sex and any age. Contacts may be casual and impermanent or deep and long-lasting. Friendship, that special sort of companionship, bonds family members or nonrelatives with strong mutual ties of support and sharing. Similar bonds exist between sexual partners and with parents and children. Although the parents can fulfill all of the social needs of an infant, the child rapidly grows beyond them and needs associations with contemporaries and other adults for complete social development. Many, but not all, parental needs are satisfied by care of the youngster.

People who can sustain a solitary life are rare. Their social needs may be somewhat less than usual, and they may be able to satisfy them by associations with other creatures and by inner strengths.

Although we have strong social needs, our social consciousness is curiously ambivalent. We need people and can deal with them easily on an individual basis or in small groups. We are not comfortable in a crowd and subconsciously employ a number of social devices to wall ourselves off from others and to provide and maintain a personal space of about two feet. If that space is invaded, we become annoyed and tend to manifest behaviors ranging from resignation to belligerence, depending both on the person and on the circumstances. We have empathy and sympathy for our fellows and may expend considerable effort in their behalf at some times, whereas at other times we are indifferent, protecting ourselves from involvement. We usually care deeply for family and close friends but may categorize whole groups of humanity whose actions we do not like as being less worthwhile or even less human than we are.

URBAN PRESSURES

The modern urban world is a human creation, which in turn profoundly affects us. It is a world of concrete and glass, light and noise, hope and despair, endless buildings and activity. It is a busy and impersonal world, crowded, yet the people are strangely lonely. Many live their entire lifetimes there, have all their material needs met, and still do not quite belong. There is an artificiality to that life that runs counter to some ingrained sense of being and belonging. For we are, like our tribal ancestors, creatures of small groups that give us a sense of belonging and identity. In a society that is becoming increasingly complex, there is an increase in all sorts of stress-related medical problems: tension, depression, heart attacks, stroke, and various psychosomatic diseases.

THE LIVING WORLD

We are also creatures of the natural world whose rhythms govern our lives, though frequently in opposition to the world in which we live. The natural world is one marked by the rhythms of daylight and darkness, of changing seasons, of new life and old, of life and death as they exist for every living thing on earth. This world, deeply ingrained in our being, speaks to each of us regardless of age or culture. It is possible to ignore this calling by insulating ourselves in the urban world of busyness, where the concerns of earning a living seem all important and even recreation is hurried, and to consider the natural world as a remote place to which we can escape occasionally. But this runs counter to our basic selves. The living world can afford some relief from the stresses of life. Expanses of greenery with assorted animals, flowing rivers, crashing surf, mountain peaks against the sky—all speak to the very depths of our being. We are a part of this natural world, and being in touch with it puts us in touch with our roots while it soothes and refreshes us. The psychological effect of nature is one of the reasons that natural areas must be preserved: we need them for our sanity. Although we need to know that open areas and wilderness exist in the world, we also need to encounter nature personally and frequently. For many people, the only encounters are with houseplants and pets, but these can be sufficient to sustain them even in stressful situations.

Many of our current problems stem from feelings of remoteness and alienation from the natural world. We need to recognize that we are part of it and dependent on it, that recognition requires feelings of humility and acceptance. We are not good at such feelings.

THE DOG

What is the dog to us? When first domesticated and for long years thereafter, the dog's role was almost exclusively utilitarian (see Chapter 11). Dogs worked; they hunted with man, guarded his property, protected his family, herded his stock. But companionship has always been a role, too; people and dogs have drifted together throughout our long association, especially children and the lonely. The primary role of the dog in modern society is that of companion.

At its best, living with a dog is a rewarding experience. The dog has many familiar emotions, all of which it expresses openly without deceit or polite cover-up. It accepts its lot in life, and its eyes mirror that life. When it has a special person who cares deeply for it, the dog gazes at that person with eyes sparkling with unquestioning devotion. Knowing one's own errors, shortcomings, and weaknesses, it is awe-inspiring to receive such pure love from another being. Few of us can so fully accept another human being.

Having a dog is a responsibility and a commitment, one that many would not wish to make. For those who do, though, this is but a small price to pay for the joy, the companionship, the opportunity to live with and learn from another kind of living creature. In fulfilling your dog's needs, you are rewarded. The walk does you both good. Time put into grooming and training pays off in the sense of pride in having an attractive, well-mannered friend. Strangers stop to admire and converse. You receive ample gratification from the association. So should the dog. It should not be regarded merely as a valuable possession, a means of gratifying an ego, but as exactly what it is: a living creature with personality and sensitivity, whom we have made dependent and must care for. Because the dog accepts what befalls it, it is easy to impose on it or to neglect it, but to do so degrades us by robbing us of some of our humanity. The relationship should always be an elevating, not demeaning, one for the person.

There is no question, though, that people who have dogs can easily become their own worst enemies by permitting them to be nuisances. This is very easy to prevent by training. The same training that builds the bond between you and your dog can prevent neighborhood problems and restrictive housing. It is a matter of caring and taking responsibility. The rights of those who do not wish to have dogs, or to be annoyed by them, need to be protected as well as those of dog owners. The two preferences should be able to coexist.

The companion dog should be friendly, intelligent, trusting, dependable, trainable, willing, and should have character. It is better to have some mischief than a flat, characterless personality. Individuality in mannerisms and habits is endearing, providing much of the source of enjoyment of dogs. The dog should be a do-anything, go-anywhere sort of friend.

The trait that is of highest priority for a companion dog is temperament (see Chapter 1), which must be stable, even, well-balanced, adaptable. An outgoing personality, a trait many people look for in a puppy, may not be the easiest to live with. The outgoing puppy in the litter is the dominant one. A strong will and stubbornness often accompany that personality, necessitating proper training early in life. If the pup does not get that, it establishes its dominance, creating behavioral problems, but with firm discipline, this dog can make a fine companion. Breeders often prefer outgoing pups for their confidence and ability to project themselves, an asset in the show ring. Sometimes, though, that is not the sort of temperament that is original, or even desirable, for the particular breed. A more submissive pup, easier to handle, can become a fine companion, too; training methods emphasize encouragement rather than firmness. Your methods should always suit the temperament of the dog.

The companion dog should also be healthy (see Chapter 1). It must be physically well built and therefore not likely to develop problems (save for accidents) during its prime years. Past puppyhood, it should not be a stumblebum, running the risk of injury in the course of ordinary living. Although physical problems normally accompany the aging process, the structurally sound dog is apt to live a longer and healthier life than one that is not. The dog should be able to live a normal life without undue medical support.

The requirements for a successful companion are subtle. The personalities of person and dog should mesh so that they are well suited to each other. Ideally, dogs should be bred for the important role of companions.

MEETING HUMAN NEEDS

Dogs are directly beneficial to humans in a number of ways. Anyone who shares life with a dog knows how much affection, happiness, security, and warmth the dog gives. Indeed, the dog positively gives a lift to life. Scientific studies now under way indicate the same thing. Most of that research is being done with handicapped people and involves the roles that dogs can play as therapeutic assistants for those with impairments and as companions for those confined to institutions.

Institutions. Life in an institution is barren at best. Most of the softening elements that lift life above existence are sacrificed to efficiency of operation and staff convenience. The hours of the day are scheduled; the schedule becomes routine; the routine becomes boring. Apathy abounds, making it more difficult to achieve success with any constructive activities. Generally, animals, and even plants, are excluded from institutions, contributing to the bleakness. Some institutions, located in the country, have long maintained farms and have expected the residents to work on them. The practice was doubtless employed with the idea that they could help earn their living, but additional benefits accrued as well. Those who cared for animals and crops were outdoors with ever-changing nature; they were exhilarated, used their bodies and minds, had something to talk about, and were physically tired after a day's work. Troubled spirits were calmed.

Medical Problems. Obviously, the dog does not cure any medical problems. It can help improve a person's outlook and thus may facilitate responses to treatment. Therapeutic uses of dogs should increase as we gain better understanding of the benefits that can result.

There are some direct medical benefits of the association. Recent studies have been done on hospital patients, following the course of their recovery both in the hospital and after they returned home. One of the factors investigated was the presence of dogs (or other companion animals) in the patient's home. It was found that the survival rate for heart attack victims was much higher for those who had pets than for those who did not and that the attitude of hospitalized pet owners was better, too. It seems that devotion to an animal and concern about its welfare have a therapeutic value; the person is eager to be out of the hospital and back at home. Mental involvement with life is beneficial for physical recovery.

The sense of touch is a more important one than we usually imagine. Small children spontaneously touch everything and learn about things by the way they feel, but, more important, touch is the sense for showing emotion and feelings. In our society, adults touching one another is not considered acceptable except between relatives or close friends; often the touch is limited to shaking hands. Touching, even cuddling, little children and animals, however, is acceptable. Many mentally retarded people, lacking the cultural taboos, openly touch strangers and show them affection. Touch, a natural human social response, may be part of ancient patterns of greeting others and receiving comfort and assurance from them, just as it is in canid packs. When a person quietly caresses and talks to a dog, they both relax with the soothing, rhythmic contact. A measure of their relaxation is that blood pressure levels are lowered for both of them. The effects on the person are more marked than with other sorts of relaxing activities, such as talking or reading, and are similar to those obtained through biofeedback and meditation techniques. The effects are greatest in children and adults who have high blood pressure.

Hospitals in various countries, most notably in Great Britain, have made a practice of keeping dogs, and the patients have enjoyed their company. The practice was seldom employed in this country, on the assumption that dogs are "dirty" and "too much work." However, as administrators become aware of the beneficial roles that dogs can play, they are increasingly being accepted in homes for the aged, nursing homes, psychiatric and correctional institutions, and those for the mentally retarded. Many of the residents are withdrawn and uncommunicative people who do not respond well to other human beings. A friendly dog is not a creature to be ignored. Even if the person's initial response to it is but a slow smile and a faltering touch, a start has been made in communication. Withdrawn people have been observed gradually taking an interest in their surroundings, themselves, others, and life in general. The dog stimulates conversation. At first the talk is about the dog, but as the people open up more with one another, additional topics of conversation are found that make life more interesting and meaningful.

Obviously, dogs cannot be used by all people. There are individuals who are unresponsive to them, just as there are those who would be cruel. Yet, these are not in the majority; seemingly, the friendly, trusting nature of the dog tends to bring out the best in people, even severely disturbed ones. Of course, not all dogs are acceptable either. Patients and dogs must be well matched for maximum mutual satisfaction.

Dogs for the Handicapped. The first known attempts to enlist canine help for handicapped people took place only about a hundred years ago, when someone tried to use a dog as a guide

This Corgi is a trained Signal Dog who acts as the ears for his deaf mistress. The baby just woke up from his nap and is crying for attention, but the mother, who cannot hear him, goes on reading. Seeing that the baby is awake, the dog will run to the mother, alerting her to the child's cry. He is also trained to respond to the other sounds of her daily life, such as the doorbell, telephone, alarm clock, teakettle, and so on by running to his mistress and leading her to the source of the sound. He also retrieves dropped objects and provides her with companionship and a sense of independence.

for a blind person. At present, the range of assistance activities is rapidly expanding as we understand canine capabilities better. Using dogs to assist the handicapped is the greatest role we have found for our canine friends.

Training programs for guide dogs were first developed about fifty years ago and have been greatly refined since then. The dogs are bred for the job and home-raised by dedicated youngsters until they are old enough to begin the exacting course of training. A fully trained and experienced guide dog sees for its human, giving the person the freedom to pursue an education, a career, and social activities. With independence comes the feeling of dignity so important to us all. The dog is also a beloved friend in an especially close relationship.

The counterpart for the deaf is of recent development. The dog is trained to alert its person to the ordinary sounds of living—doorbell, telephone, crying child, smoke detector, alarm clock—by nuzzling or by running back and forth between the person and the source of the sound. The dogs are also trained to retrieve dropped objects that the person does not hear falling. Here, too, dogs provide independence and friendship to their people.

Some assistance dogs walk beside wheelchairs, carrying packs, helping to pull the chair up steep inclines. They can also be taught to open doors, push elevator buttons, and bring needed objects. This is a new area of usefulness for the dog.

Handicapped people often feel particularly vulnerable, both on the streets and in their homes. A dog gives them a sense of security as well as companionship.

Therapy dogs for many of these programs are donated by interested breeders or rescued from pounds. They are intelligent and willing, large or small, purebred or not, and past puppyhood when they begin training for the job.

Why is it that the dog, of all domestic animals, is so able to provide for human needs? In all probability, the major reason is that both are social creatures with many common social needs.

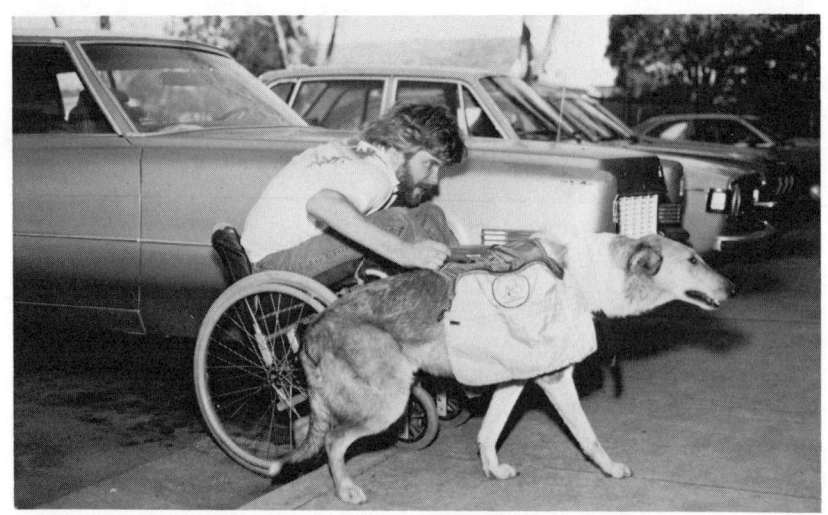

Joker is a Service Dog who provides freedom for his master. Not only does he pull the wheelchair over the curb, he also carries needed possessions in his backpack, picks up objects, and assists in numerous other ways with his large vocabulary of over eighty different commands.

Ivy, another Service Dog, is calling for the elevator for her nine-year-old, wheelchair-bound master. She is his constant companion. She turns lights on and off, gets things he can't reach, brings his clothes in the morning, sleeps with him at night, and goes to school.

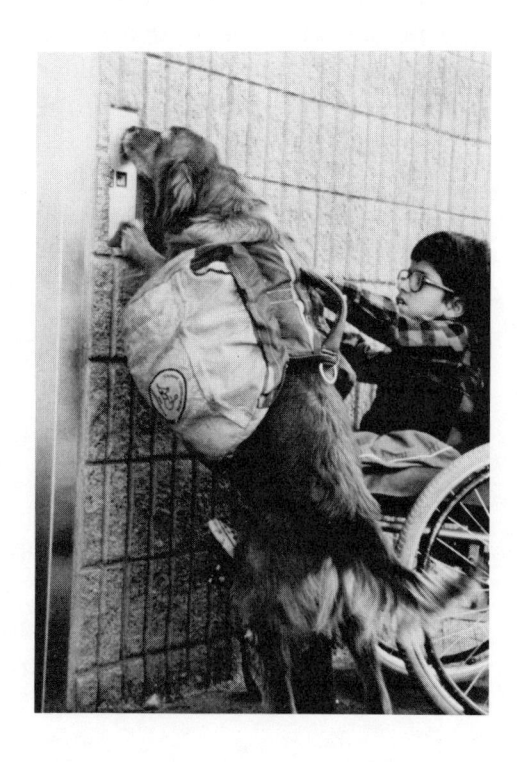

The dog is an eager, loyal, intelligent, responsive creature. Because it remembers, it can be trained to obey and to follow directions. More important, it has the ability to disobey commands when circumstances warrant. A blind person may direct his dog to go forward; the guide dog must use its judgment to determine when it is safe to proceed and what route is to be taken around the hazards of the area. The dog takes responsibility and makes decisions—these are the acts of a thinking being, not merely the result of training. All types of therapy dogs sense the person's handicap and the resultant dependency and assume the leadership role, which the person must learn to accept and to trust. No other animal is capable of that.

Children and Dogs. Some therapy programs are offering obedience-training classes for physically handicapped or emotionally disturbed children. The youngsters are taught how to train their dogs, putting them into a leadership position, often for the first time in their lives. The rewards to the child in terms of ability to communicate and teach, self-confidence, willingness to think of others first, and just plain fun are enormous and clearly worthwhile.

Many of the dog's traits are qualities that we consider desirable for our children: love, loyalty, devotion to duty, caring, and sharing. A canine companion can be a good educator for a child. When they are properly raised with discipline for both child and dog, the youngster learns valuable lessons: to care for a dependent creature (a good preparation for parenthood), humaneness, reverence for life, acceptance of death. The dog is fun, besides.

The dog has been with us as long as human civilization. We need it now for the gentling effect it can have on us if we will but let it. After all, any creature that can make a dejected person smile *must* be a highly commendable one. Perhaps we may come to see the dog as a necessity in life and will protect the right of a person to share his life with one.

11

The Dog's History

In order to understand your dog better, you should know something about canine origins and history, including the ways wild animals were altered to suit human purposes.

THE ORIGIN OF THE DOG

The association of people and dogs stretches back thousands of years, before the dawning of civilization, when our ancestors adopted some helpless, orphan pups—probably young wolves. They accepted scraps tossed at them, possibly even a furtive outstretched hand reaching toward and even touching them. As they grew up around the camp, the pups would regard it as their home. When they were half-grown and their behavior developed, they would begin to defend the area, snarling at intruders, frightening them away. Clearly, people would have been afraid of the fiercer animals and probably killed them or drove them off, while allowing the more docile ones to remain around the campsite. This act of disposing of the more aggressive animals while permitting the less aggressive ones to remain and then to breed was the first act of altering animals to suit human desires. The road toward the development of the dog had begun.

It probably took a while for the real possibilities of the association to dawn on people. The animals defended the camp and alerted humans to danger. They tagged along on hunting expeditions, and men discovered that hunting with them was more effective than hunting alone. Thus began the cooperation between humans and canines and two important roles that dogs have served ever since—the guardian and the hunter.

Dogs themselves are not creatures of the wild but are descended from a mix of several canids, particularly the wolf, coyote, jackal, and an extinct canid, which were selectively bred by humans. Coyotes and jackals are smaller than wolves and usually are solitary animals lacking a social organization such as wolves have. Wolves have (*had* is more correct) the more extensive range, covering the Northern Hemisphere, whereas coyotes and jackals have more limited habitats, generally at the southern parts of the wolf range. However, the wolf is the principal progenitor of the dog. Wolves are intelligent animals with complicated behavioral patterns that make possible a complex social organization. Their behavior, important to understanding dog behavior, is discussed in the next section.

WOLVES

Wolves live in family groups or packs. A pack is made up of a pair of wolves and some of their offspring, a small band of six to eight members. It is formed initially either by lone individuals of opposite sexes joining forces, or by an orphaned litter that remains together.

The group is highly organized. The top-ranking animals, both male and female, are the leaders, with the rest of the pack subordinate to them. These individuals are the original pair or the most dominant members of the litter. Dominance depends to some extent on size and age, but even more on strength of character. A dominant animal is assertive and simply cannot be ignored; those that are less forceful stand back and defer to it. In time, the dominant animal assumes the leadership position—usually neither easily nor permanently.

The most dominant male is the pack's leader. He maintains order and is the dictator, guide, and teacher as circumstances require. The other males, his sons, are subordinate to him and may show some dominance among themselves. Of several males in a litter, there are variations in assertiveness, with some being quite assertive and others less so. The most assertive male becomes the leader of the litter and, as he grows up, may assume the second ranking position in the pack next to his father. The young lieutenant usually challenges his father for leadership.

The dominant female, sometimes even more assertive than the dominant male, ranks below him but is capable of taking over the leadership of the pack if he should die. Her daughters are all subordinate to her.

The dominant female is bred on each of her annual heat cycles. The leader is her mate for some years, although in time the second ranking male may take over that role. Thus, with wolves, breeding rights are not necessarily the exclusive privilege of leadership. Young males are all interested in the dominant female and engage in nudging, nuzzling, and other forms of sexual play with her. Mounting and actual mating, however, are limited to the two top males. Not all of the females are bred. The more assertive ones are, but submissive ones often do not engage in sexual behavior and usually are not bred. The actual number of breeding animals in the pack thus is quite limited.

Wolves are territorial animals. They seek shelter in rock crevasses and other natural den areas and then stake out the surrounding territory as their own, marking the borders with urine and patrolling and defending the area against other packs. The pups are born in the den and remain in it while nursing. When they are no longer dependent on their mother, the whole pack takes over the care, feeding, training, and protection of the pups. Subordinates are left in charge of them

These animals are wolves. While they resemble dogs, it is apparent that they are a different kind of animal. These two are males and their expressions communicate a great deal about their relationship and their moods. The younger animal is on the left. He is not quite so heavy as the older one, nor has he has much coat, but he is prepared to challenge the other. His fixed and penetrating stare is an act of aggression toward the more dominant animal. The older male meets this challenge with a warning. The fur on his neck and the top of his head is ruffled, his face muscles contract, making the eyebrows more prominent, and he glances at his rival from under them. The skin at the top of the muzzle wrinkles in the beginning of a threatening snarl. He pushes against his challenger with his shoulder; the younger male, leaning slightly, has begun to give way.

when the others take off on hunting expeditions. Unlike dogs, only the leader marks his territory by lifting his leg to urinate. This gesture is, therefore, a sign of higher social status. If the leader discovers a urine marking from another pack's leader, he will overprint the spot with his own urine, thus claiming the territory as his own (see Chapter 3).

The leader continually demonstrates his leadership by putting down any challenges to his authority, both from within his pack and from neighboring pack leaders.

Within the pack, the leader administers the discipline that keeps the group in line. His primary tactics are eye contact and interference. When he makes eye contact, he fixes the subordinate with a penetrating stare (see Chapter 3). The subordinate, unable to meet that gaze for long, looks away. Interfering with a subordinate's activities is done by shouldering it out of the way, by standing astride its prostrate body, or by seizing its muzzle, forcing it to the ground, and holding the underling down. The disciplined one lowers its body, avoiding the leader's eyes, and gets out of his way. With young pups, the leader grabs the scruff of the neck in his mouth and gives it a good shake (see Chapter 5). The pup squeals loudly. Released, the pup goes up to him, holding its head up, ears folded back humbly, tail low and wagging, holding out a paw in supplication. The leader turns his head aside, his expression soft and kindly.

Subordinates accept the chastisement and defer to the dominant animal. The young learn proper pack conduct and respect for authority. Even though subordinates are disciplined several times during a day, they are not cowed. Discipline is prompt; so is forgiveness. Subordinates are only secure when there is a strong leader in charge of a structured and controlled society.

The leader spends most of his time watching. His ears are up, eyes alert, mouth closed, fur smooth over his head and body. When another individual approaches with an air of challenge, his whole countenance changes rapidly. His head snaps up to catch the full impact of sensations. The hackles rise on back and neck. The skin over the skull contracts (like furrowing of the brow), ruffling the fur and bringing the ears angled forward sharply. The eyes appear darker and glare ominously. The skin of the muzzle wrinkles, and the mouth gapes open, exposing the teeth. The tail is held up, straight and motionless. Muscles are taut, ready for action. The tightened muscles of the legs make the action stiff, the stride short. A deep rumbling growl accompanies the threatening body pose. He exudes menace.

The first part of an encounter is ceremonial. The two individuals approach stiff-legged, presenting their sides toward one another. They stand tall on their stiff legs with fur ruffled out, which makes them appear large and impressive. In many cases, this posturing is sufficient. One individual, usually the junior, recognizing his inferiority, simply accedes. In doing so, he turns his head aside and lowers his gaze; the skin smooths over muzzle, skull, and back, and the coat flattens. Ears fold back into the ruff, the eyes become slits, the mouth closes. The tail drops. Muscle tension diminishes and body posture is lowered. The animal slinks away, making itself as small as possible.

If, however, one does not give way, the course is set toward a fight. The combatants stand shoulder to shoulder. They circle each other, measuring. The scene is noisy with snapping jaws and thundering growls. Each tries to grab the other and flip him over. They aim for legs, ears, and neck. Each presents the side of the neck, thick with muscle and fur, to make grappling difficult. Each protects his throat by turning his head aside or lowering it. If neither gives way, eventually one of them will be brought down or the throat grabbed. This usually signals the end of the fight. Often, the one that feels himself losing will go down on his own, lying on his back at the feet of his adversary. It happens in an instant. At one moment, the fight is waged at full intensity; at the next, one contestant lies defeated. The victor does not, however, seize the golden moment to do in his victim. Instead, he is frozen, growling but unable to attack. The sight of this animal, lying on his back like a helpless puppy, inhibits him. The victor seems puzzled. He continues to stand over the victim, muttering. Gradually his intensity cools, especially if aided by pathetic whimpers from the victim. He stalks off. The victim slinks away. Their relationship is established. They know their positions.

Wolves are hunters that prey on the large, grazing herd animals of their particular part of the world. Although wolves are smaller and much slower, they substitute strategy for speed. For them, hunting is a group activity, and wolves are very efficient hunters. The pack ranges widely in search of its prey and locates a herd either visually or by following a scent trail. The individual wolves fan out, surrounding the herd at some distance, silently stalking or slinking ever closer. Once some members of the herd sense danger, the group is alerted and flees, with the wolves running beside and behind them, driving them ahead. During the drive, the wolves take the measure of the herd, singling out its weaker members. By combined effort, the pack cuts one weak individual from the group. It is surrounded and isolated, attacked from one side and then the other. Confused, wounded, and exhausted, it becomes an easy victim. At the opportune moment, one wolf lunges for the throat and brings the prey down. It is killed. All the pack members participate in tearing at the body and eating. Some portions of the kill are carried back to the pack's den afterward.

When the pack returns after a hunting expedition, those that remained at the den greet them with great shows of affection, nuzzling, pawing, and licking them in welcome.

DOG BREEDING AND SELECTION

Dogs do not have all the same behaviors, or to the same extent, as wolves, but having some common heritage, they share many behavioral traits and can communicate with each other. Wolves have a wider range of behaviors, both instinctive and learned, and more diverse means of communication than do dogs. They are also more predictable and consistent. The behavioral system of the wolf, stabilized during its history, has been broken up in the dog as a result of breeding for specific purposes.

Early Domestication. The dog has existed as a distinct type of animal for ten thousand to eleven thousand years—our first domestic creature. Remains of these early dogs are found with human remains around ancient campsites, but older canid fossils that have been found cannot be categorized so easily. So similar is the early dog's skeleton to that of the wolf that it can best be identified by its association with human evidences.

In the early stages of domestication, canids hung around human campsites, and selection was first practiced by disposing of the wildest animals. Those allowed to remain were the ones that our ancestors could live with. The camp followers bred with wild canids for thousands of years while the dogs were half wild or partly domesticated. It undoubtedly took a long time before dogs were completely domesticated, with humans caring for them and controlling their breeding. Later, when humans learned to control breeding, they deliberately made crosses, keeping some pups and discarding others. Animals were chosen for practical reasons: not too aggressive to handle, strong, healthy, and able to work.

The earliest trait to be selected in breeding was hunting ability. By selective breeding, the wolf hunting sequence was broken up to produce working dogs specialized in some part of the sequence. The *sighthounds,* bred from the searching component, have the most acute vision of any dog, enabling them to see the prey afar. They are great runners and hunt by running the prey down. The ability to follow a scent trail was utilized in the development of the *scenthounds* with their acute sense of smell. Like their ancestors, most of them hunt in packs. The stalking portion was used in developing the bird dogs. Further refinements were made by creating specialist dogs that stalked,

SPECIALIZED TYPES OF
DOGS DEVELOPED BY
THE BREAKUP OF THE
WOLVES' HUNTING
SEQUENCE THROUGH
SELECTIVE BREEDING.

Sighthounds are derived from the searching component (Saluki).

Scenthounds are specialized to follow a scent trail (Beagle).

Bird dogs are derived from the stalking component (Brittany).

Herding dogs are specialized in the cutting and driving segment (Border Collie).

Terriers are derived from the attacking component (Border Terrier).

Retrievers are specialized to carry off the prey (Labrador Retriever).

FRIENDSHIP: YOU AND YOUR DOG

pointed, or flushed birds from their hiding places. The driving and cutting parts of the sequence were used by farmers who bred herding dogs. The herders, like their ancestors, employ stalking and slinking to collect a flock or herd, move it where desired, and cut out particular individuals. The attack-and-kill components, inhibited in many dogs, were retained in the terriers, which were bred to "go to ground" in pursuit of "varmints" and to dispatch them. Retrievers, developed after the invention of guns, were bred to capitalize on the last part of the hunting sequence. They bring the kill back to the hunter, though, not to the den.

Uses for the Dog. In addition to those working dogs, dogs have been developed for several other purposes.

In addition to hunting and its derived roles, the other major use of the dog is as a guardian. Some breeds have been developed specifically as guards; the dogs are large and look imposing. Some of them have long been used for protection and attack as military or police dogs.

Still other uses, not related to the dog's natural behavior, show canine versatility. Dogs have been used as draft animals to pull travois, sleds, and carts or to carry panniers since ancient times. In addition, dogs have been used for racing, fighting, rescue, exhibition, carrying messages, seeking out contraband, as a source of food, or in a combination of several roles. Humanitarian roles, mentioned in Chapter 10, are of recent development.

Some diminutive dogs were always bred exclusively for companionship, though scorn has often been heaped on them as pampered pets, "not good for anything." But in modern times, most dogs do not do the work for which their kind was originally bred. The dog's prime role is now that of a companion—the role most rewarding for the dog.

Breeding Practices. In order to develop a breed, dogs having the desired characteristics are bred together and only the offspring also possessing those traits are used for breeding. Quality is maintained through rigorous selection, and in time the animals become more uniform in their appearance and behavior. They are considered purebred dogs when breeding has taken place only within the particular breed for many generations. There are a number of very ancient breeds whose lineages can be traced back thousands of years, for example, the Saluki, Greyhound, Ibizan Hound, Mastiff, Cardigan Welsh Corgi, Norwegian Elkhound, Maltese, Chow Chow, Tibetan Terrier, and Basenji. These originated in widely scattered parts of the world and indicate that humans have practiced selective breeding for a long time.

Showing dogs as a means of comparing different animals and selecting breeding stock is quite recent (1859). Breeders' associations were formed later to preserve (and sometimes promote) a particular breed. One of the prime functions of the association is to compose an agreed-on standard that describes the ideal dog of the breed. The standard then becomes the focal point for breeding and showing.

Nowadays many breeders breed for the show ring, with the result that selection has shifted from practical considerations to physical attractiveness and a showman's personality. Shows have assumed too much importance for them. The bigger the winner, the more it will be bred, and the more surely its offspring will be crossed together in an attempt to re-create or improve on the original winner. There is a great deal of publicity and promotion for the top winners and producers. Dogs are valuable animals.

One might question current breeding practices, though, as undesirable traits begin to appear more frequently. Earlier breeding practices allowed animals with undesirable traits to die, but increasingly now every effort is made to keep them alive with the latest medical procedures, often with the result that they are used for breeding. This sort of practice results in an increase in the number of undesirable, or detrimental, traits in a breed. Rigorous selection of breeding stock, the breeders' hallmark for thousands of years, has been allowed to slacken by the fainthearted. Purebred dogs, especially the currently popular breeds, have in some instances deteriorated by the accumulation of such traits.

Always there have been breeders of the highest integrity who have practiced their art in conscience, to the best of their knowledge. They are to be found for every breed and are passionately devoted to it. In every breed, too, are the charlatans, the profiteers, and the ignorant. They are not genuine breeders.

A Final Word

I wish for you a dog to love and to share your life. I wish you to gain from that friendship in more ways than you ever dreamed possible. When your dog dies, I want you to cry for your loss, for the shortness of that life that meant so much and that gave you so much. Grieve for your wonderful friend. And when your sorrow has abated somewhat, begin again with a brand-new dog, whose ways are delightfully different and whose joy of life bounces you back into the fullness of living. Remember the old fondly, but go on with the new. Pause occasionally in the busyness of your life to look back on all those friends who have shared it at different times. From each you learned. To each you are grateful.

Appendix 1

Reproduction and Prenatal Development

Reproduction in the dog is controlled by the female's heat cycles. These take place, with a considerable amount of variability, about every six months. The heat period lasts for about three weeks and is regulated by different hormones that are responsible for the ripening of eggs in the ovary, their release in ovulation, preparation of the uterus for pregnancy, and sexual behavior. It is only during the estrus period, in the middle of the heat, that the female will mate. The average time of ovulation is the twelfth day of the heat, again with considerable individual variation. Females are usually eagerly receptive during the period from about the tenth to the sixteenth day. Following that, the hormone levels gradually diminish, and, as they do, the female becomes less and less interested in breeding. Finally, about the end of the third week, she goes out of heat and enters the longest portion of her cycle, between heats. The hormone levels are low at that time, and normally there is no sexual activity.

PRENATAL DEVELOPMENT

Prenatal development in the dog lasts about sixty days and is divided into three periods.

The Ovum. After mating, the sperm require several hours to travel up the uterus to the oviducts at the upper ends of the reproductive tract, where fertilization takes place. Frequently, there are delays of several days before development actually begins. These delays can be due to mating before ovulation or before the eggs (*ova*) are ready to be fertilized. Gestation is more nearly nine weeks, including the delays, but the average length of actual development is sixty days. The new life begins when egg and sperm unite.

Soon after this the ovum begins to divide. Cell divisions convert the single-celled ovum into a cluster of tiny cells. While cell division is taking place, the cluster (still called an *ovum*) is being moved down the oviducts to the uterus. Transport takes about a week. At first, the cluster is a solid little ball of cells; later the cells gradually spread apart, forming a single-layered ring of cells with a solid group of them at one end. That "signet-ring" stage, called a *blastocyst,* floats in the uterus for several days. By the seventeenth to eighteenth day, the blastocysts become spread out along the length of the uterus and begin to implant in its wall. The beinning of implantation marks the end of the first developmental period.

The Embryo. The second period, which lasts from the seventeenth to the thirty-fourth day of development, is the stage in which the organs of the body are formed. The greatest changes take place during these seventeen days.

The first major event is *implantation.* The floating blastocysts drift into small indentations in the wall of the uterus. The cellular ring grows by cell division, and the new cells grow into the tissues of the uterus. Literally, the blastocyst invades its mother's body and obtains its nutrients from her tissues. The

APPENDIX 1

cells of the ring are supportive and give rise to the membranes that surround the embryo and to the placenta. The group of cells inside the ring becomes the embryo itself. Implantation is crucial in order to establish the embryo's supply line.

Once implantation is under way, embryonic develpment proceeds rapidly. The inner group of cells flattens out and then rearranges itself by the movement of cells. A three-cell-layered disk results, which then elongates into an oval shape. The layers break into blocks of cells that then rough out the primary shapes of the first structures of the body. The nervous system, the first system to develop, forms as a flat plate running the length of the body. The plate's edges then roll inward and meet to form the *neural tube*, the forerunner of the brain and spinal cord. On either side of the developing nervous system, square blocks of cells (*somites*) appear, starting at the head end and adding on toward the rear. They give rise to vertebrae and muscles. First appearing on day nineteen to twenty, somites are added rapidly thereafter.

The twenty-one-day embryo is crescent-shaped, with sixteen somites, the beginnings of a brain and heart, and is five millimeters (about one-fifth inch) long.* The twenty-three-day embryo is twice as long and has twice as many somites as the twenty-one-day-old. Limbs first appear as bulges on the sides of the body. Ears, eyes, jaw, digestive tract, and liver are also forming. By twenty-five days, the somites begin to develop into vertebrae, and no new ones are added. The limbs have grown out, and their ends are flattened into paddles that will become the paws. Muscles are developing on the body and limbs. There is a sharp bend at the back of the head that tips it forward, so that the top of the head nearly meets the tip of the tail and the body is curled into a small ball.

*Measurements are from the top of the head to the end of the rump, tail not included. They are given in millimeters and inches (twenty-five millimeters equals approximately one inch). Information and measurements are taken from Evans's study of the Beagle: Howard E. Evans, "Reproduction and Prenatal Development," in *Miller's Anatomy of the Dog*, by Howard E. Evans and George C. Christensen (Philadelphia: W. B. Saunders Co., 1979): Chap. 2.

REPRODUCTION AND PRENATAL DEVELOPMENT

On the twenty-first day, a bulge forms from the end of the digestive tract. It grows outward rapidly to form a sac that contacts the embryo's outermost membrane (*chorion*). These two embryonic structures in combination with uterine tissues become the *placenta,* the exchange area between the bloodstreams of mother and embryo. Here, nutrients and oxygen pass into the embryo's blood and wastes leave it. The twenty-five-day embryo has a placenta fully formed and functioning, with an umbilical cord going from it to the embryo. There are well-developed blood vessels within the embryo's body, and the heart, the first organ to function, is pumping blood. The embryo is fourteen millimeters (about one-half inch) long.

The thirty-day embryo has wide-open eyes with lids just beginning to form, a flap that projects over the ear openings, whiskers, toes on the forepaws, scalloped-edged paddles on the hindpaws, five pairs of nipples, and a genital protrusion. Sex organs have not yet developed.

The first bone forms in the skeleton at twenty-eight days and continues to form throughout the prenatal period and well into the juvenile stage of postnatal development.

The Fetus. The last period of development is the time from thirty-five to sixty days, or birth. At thirty-five days, development has proceeded to the point that the embryo is recognizable as a dog; from then on it is referred to as a *fetus.* The fetal period is one of developmental refinements and a great deal of growth. The length of the thirty-five-day fetus is thirty-five millimeters (about one and one-half inches) and at birth is one hundred sixty to one hundred seventy-five millimeters (approximately six and one-half to seven inches), or a fivefold increase in twenty-five days.

At thirty-days, the sex of the fetus can be recognized. The eyelids lengthen and almost cover the eyes, giving it a sleepy expression. By forty days, the lids meet and fuse. The eyes are then closed for the next thirty-five days while finishing touches are put on their development. Flaps close over the ear openings

APPENDIX 1

at thirty-five days; the ear canal gradually closes during its final development. Claws are present on all toes by forty days. Color markings and body hair first appear at forty-five days. The scrotum develops after forty-five days, and in many males, the testes descend into it before birth. It is, however, quite common for descent not to occur until several weeks after birth.

The body of the fetus gradually straightens out, with the head in line with the back and no longer tipped forward. By fifty days, the body has filled out and is proportioned as the newborn. The fetus gains in size and in the structural refinements that enable it to breathe and to nurse once it is born (see Chapter 2).

Appendix 2

Puppy Evaluation

Many people are interested in trying to determine the natural aptitudes of young puppies, hoping that they can find a means of predicting the temperament and abilities of the mature dog. Clearly, it is very desirable to be able to screen pups and predict potential success before undertaking long and expensive training for particular jobs. Several different puppy tests have been devised, some very specific, others more general, attempting to evaluate the desirable qualities for a companion dog.

You should be aware that no test can guarantee you the perfect companion. Tests are always imperfect, and so is their administration, and the puppy itself is not a fully formed entity but rather a creature in flux. The brain has just completed its physical development (see Chapter 2), and the pup is almost completely inexperienced with the world. In terms of personality, it is practically unformed. Much of its temperament and personality depend on experiences and opportunities to learn that are still to come. What the tests can do is to give you *clues* that reveal natural behavior to help you select and train your puppy.

* * *

APPENDIX 2

This puppy evaluation test is one that I developed and use, incorporating some of the individual tests used and described by William E. Campbell, Melissa Bartlett, and Lois Meistrell* (see also References), with modifications and additions. There are ten short tests designed to give some indication of basic temperament, soundness, responsiveness, and willingness to learn. The puppy is rated on each test according to its responses as excellent (E), good (G), fair (F), and poor (P). Further explanation of each test is included under "Comment."

The puppies must be at least forty-nine days old (seven weeks). Before that they have not developed sufficiently to give valid results (see Chapter 2). Read over the tests and collect everything you need before starting. Choose a quiet and confined place (a room or yard) that is unfamiliar to the pups. One or two persons should do all the testing. The tester should be able to treat all the puppies in the same calm, methodical way, without favoritism. Try not to have any distractions to confuse the issue; do not include small children in the proceedings. The puppies must be rested and alert; move through the tests quickly so that the puppy does not get tired. For the most reliable evaluation, test the whole litter, one by one, even if you are only interested in one sex or color. If this is a litter of look-alike pups, tie different-colored ribbons around their necks for identification.

1. STRUCTURE

Purpose: To determine sound structure. Note: The criteria apply to most, but not all, breeds. The breeder should be helpful about the variations of a particular breed. Structure does not improve with age, and unsoundness becomes aggravated as the dog gets older. This can limit activities.

---

*Melissa Bartlett, "A Novice Looks at Puppy Aptitude Testing," *Pure-Bred Dogs/American Kennel Gazette* (March 1979); William E. Campbell, *Behavior Problems in Dogs* (American Veterinary Publications, Inc., Drawer KK, Santa Barbara, CA 93102); Lois Meistrell, "Al and Mona," *Progress*, Quarterly Newsletter, Gaines Dog Research Center (Spring 1982).

PUPPY EVALUATION

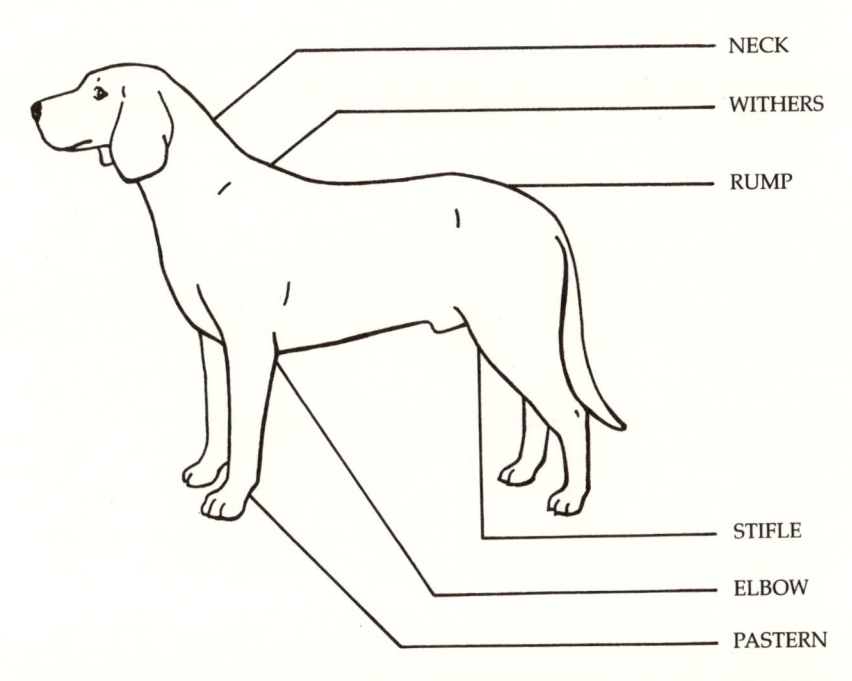

- NECK
- WITHERS
- RUMP
- STIFLE
- ELBOW
- PASTERN

The important structures to look for in evaluating the puppy are indicated on this outline drawing.

Procedure: Have a table, crate, or box in the testing area. It should stand firmly without rocking and have a nonskid surface. Put the puppy on it and gently ease it up into its natural stance. It may need reassurance and propping. Look for the following and compare with the drawing above.

    a. When viewed from the front and from the rear, the legs are straight.
    b. The neck is arched with the head carried high.
    c. The elbow is in line with the withers.
    d. The stifle is long and curved.
    e. If the palm of one hand is placed flat on the rump, it slopes backward slightly.
    f. The pastern slopes backward very slightly.
    g. In motion (see test 3), the hind feet are directly in line with

APPENDIX 2

the front feet. The legs do not twist or swing to the sides, but tend to come in under the body.

Results	Rating
Excellent structure, moves very well	E
Slightly off in one part, moves well	G
Slightly off in two or more parts, moves fairly well	F
Extreme deviation in one or several parts, front out of balance with rear, moves poorly	P

Comment. The best choices are E and G, with F being acceptable if otherwise desirable. P should not be chosen.

2. SENSITIVITY TO TOUCH

Purpose: To determine responses to touch.

Procedure: While the pup is still standing on the table, crate, or box, lightly brush along its back.

Results	Rating
Acceptance	E
Excited, jumps, attempts to lick	G
Resistance, struggles	F
Fearful	P

Comment. Best choices are E and G. F may be shy and can be helped by encouragement and exposure to new situations. The fearful pup tries to hide, stays close to the tester, cringes, or whimpers. It should not be chosen.

PUPPY EVALUATION

3. EXPLORATORY BEHAVIOR

Purpose: To determine responses to strange places, curiosity, and interest.

Procedure: Put the puppy on the floor or ground. Watch its behavior and how it moves (see test 1). Do not influence the pup by talking. Do not proceed until the pup is comfortable with the area, which will take several minutes.

Results	Rating
Lively, curious, investigates	E
Hesitant, then investigates	G
More hesitant, investigates cautiously	F
Fearful	P

Comment. Best choices are E and G. F may be shy and can be helped by encouragement and exposure to new situations. The fearful pup tries to hide, stays close to the tester, cringes or whimpers. It should not be chosen.

4. AUDITORY SENSITIVITY

Purpose: To determine responses to startling sounds.

Procedure: Once the pup has accepted the testing area, use a sharp sound, such as a whistle or banging a pan with a metal spoon, to determine the responses to sound.

Results	Rating
Alert, curious, investigates	E
Alert, turns toward sound	G
Alert, fearful	F
No response	P

APPENDIX 2

Comment. Some dogs are extremely sound-sensitive and may be afraid of a sudden, loud noise. They should get over the fear quickly and not be so startled with a repeated sound. Fear is shown by crouching or trying to hide. Barking may accompany being startled. The dominant pup raises its tail while barking, whereas the submissive one carries its tail down, sometimes between its legs. The puppy that shows no response may not be able to hear or may not be curious. Neither is desirable. P should not be chosen.

5. VISUAL SENSITIVITY

Purpose: To determine responses to startling sights.

Procedure: Use a windup toy or a brightly colored plastic bag, tied with string, and jerk it across the floor in front of the pup. The motion should be abrupt and near enough so that the pup sees the object.

Results	*Rating*
Alert, curious	E
Alert, watches	G
Alert, fearful	F
No response	P

Comment. Here, too, some dogs are afraid when startled, but they should get over that quickly. Fear is manifested in the same way as on the preceding test. Barking may also accompany being startled, with similar tail carriage for dominant and submissive pups. In addition, the dominant pup often tries to attack the object. With both tests four and five, the fearful pup can be helped by more acquaintance with fear-producing situations. Again, the pup that shows no response is demonstrating undesirable behavior, for several possible reasons, and should not be chosen.

6. DISCOMFORT SENSITIVITY

Purpose: To determine responses to an uncomfortable situation.

Procedure: Sit down, holding the puppy in your lap. With your thumb and finger, press the web between two of its front toes. Apply sufficient pressure to elicit a response and immediately release the pressure when the puppy indicates that it is uncomfortable. Do not distract it by talking, or coddle it afterward.

Results	*Rating*
Feels, accepts, forgives	E
Feels, struggles, forgives	G
Feels, fearful, forgives	F
No response or aggression	P

Comment. This is not a painful situation. The pup should feel the pressure, react to it but get over that quickly, and evidence willingness to forgive by ingratiating itself (cuddling up or licking). A kind word afterward is sufficient to make E and G forget the incident; F requires more reassurance, but any of the three would make acceptable choices. P would not. No response to the amount of pressure causing a response in other pups indicates insensitivity. Acts of aggression, such as snapping, growling, or biting, are overreactions—an undesirable defense reaction. Such dogs are difficult to live with or to train.

7. COMING

Purpose: To determine responsiveness, willingness, and dependence.

Procedure: Set the pup in the testing area and take a few steps. Crouch and encourage the puppy to come by calling and hand clapping.

APPENDIX 2

Results   *Rating*

Results	Rating
Came without hesitation, wagging tail	E
Came diffidently, wagging tail	G
Stood where set down, or went away	F
No response	P

Comment. Watch tail carriage. Happy pups wag theirs. Dominant ones carry their tails stiffly erect, and submissive pups carry theirs down. The more dominant ones also jump up, paw, nibble, or lick. Not coming or going away is a sign of independence and is not so desirable. The pup that does not respond at all is indifferent or fearful.

8. TAGGING ALONG

Purpose: To determine attraction to a person, and dependence.

Procedure: While the puppy is watching you, stand up and walk off at your usual pace.

Results	Rating
Tagged along willingly	E
Followed diffidently	G
Stayed in same place, or went away	F
No response	P

Comment. Again tail carriage indicates degree of dominance. Nipping and interference are also signs of dominant behavior. Not following or going away again indicates independence, and no response denotes indifference or fearfulness.

PUPPY EVALUATION

9. WILLINGNESS TO TAKE RESTRICTIONS

Purpose: To determine the degree of dominance or submission and responses to restraint.

Procedure: Sit or kneel beside the pup and ease it into a down position. Gently roll it over so that it is lying on its back. With your hand on the puppy's chest hold it in this position for thirty seconds. Watch the puppy.

RESTRAINT TEST.

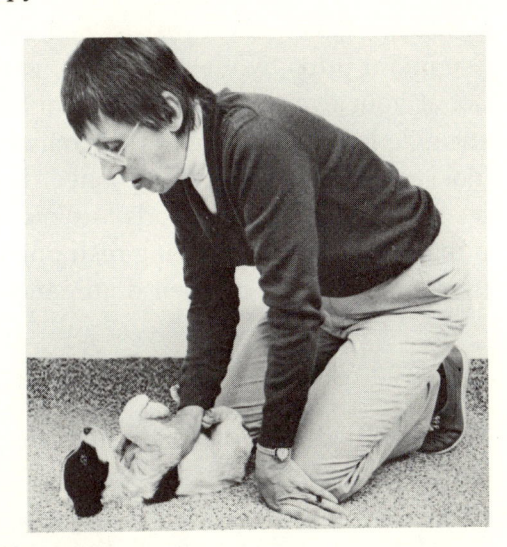

This is a dominant puppy.

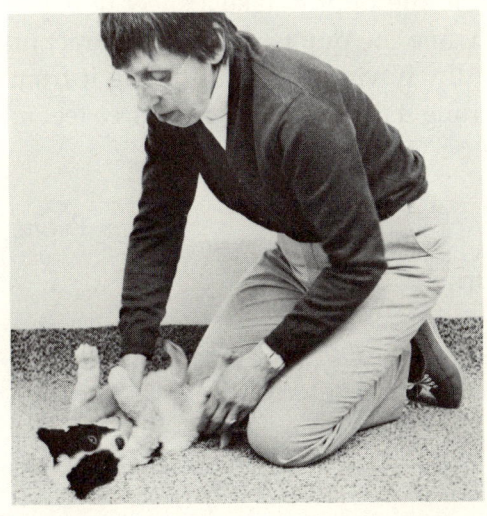

This one is submissive.

APPENDIX 2

Results   *Rating*

Squirmed, resisted some, then accepted, relaxed   E

Squirmed, resisted more, then accepted, relaxed   G

Great deal of resistance or no acceptance   F

Resisted strongly or froze, no squirming or
    resistance   P

Comment. Watch the eyes as well as the amount of activity. Dominant pups, while struggling, will look up at you (usually not at your eyes). They may attempt to bite. Submissive pups struggle less or not at all. They may have some eye contact or look aside. Very submissive ones, however, freeze rigidly in position and turn their heads to avoid eye contact. Independent pups are disturbed by being restrained and are apt to bite or to freeze, depending on their dominance or submissiveness.

10. RETRIEVING

Purpose: To determine natural retrieving ability, willingness, and responsiveness.

Procedure: Sit or kneel next to the puppy. Take a sheet of paper and crumple it into a ball while the pup is watching. Attract its attention by talking excitedly, waving the ball, tossing it from hand to hand, and then letting it drop about two to three feet in front of the pup. It must be watching.

Results: *Rating*

Goes after, picks up, returns   E

Goes after, picks up, goes away   G

Goes after, does not pick up, loses interest   F

No interest   P

Comment. This is an important test for dogs that are to be used in service work where retrieving is necessary. Because it measures a pup's desire to work with a person, it is a good measure of training aptitude. However, not all breeds take to retrieving. Some pups that show no interest in the test later do retrieve, even without formal training. Retrieving is fun for a companion dog but is not a necessity.

When you finish testing a puppy, make a fuss over it before going on to the next one. Cuddle, pet, talk happily, and give it a treat. The puppy should be happy with all the attention.

Set up a simple score sheet like this so that you can compare the pups.

TEST	1	2	3	4	5
Structure					
Sensitivity to Touch					
Exploratory Behavior					
Auditory Sensitivity					
Visual Sensitivity					
Discomfort Sensitivity					
Coming					
Tagging Along					
Willingness to Take Restrictions					
Retrieving					

Which one is your best choice? That depends on you, your family, your location, your life, as well as the basic temperament and the abilities of the dog. The results, if taken together,

APPENDIX 2

give a good indication of the dog's attributes. Generally, a dog is fairly consistent from one test to the next. If the results are inconsistent, the puppy may have been tired or have had an off-day, or perhaps there was a quirk in giving the test itself. Retest that puppy in another day or two.

Dominant pups are usually bright, outgoing, and active. They may be too active for small living quarters and are not good bets for the inexperienced, youngsters, or older people. An experienced person can train such a dog by using firmness and consistency; as you win the dog's respect and acceptance of your leadership, you develop a fine companion. Because so much training is physical, dominant dogs that are also insensitive or supersensitive to touch and to discomfort are particularly difficult to train. So are those that tend to respond quickly and aggressively to sensations, even minor ones. They are not dogs for beginners.

An exceedingly submissive puppy, at the opposite end of the spectrum, is unsure of itself, is fearful of the new, does not respond well to confusion, and is not adaptable. It can panic easily. This dog needs someone whom it can trust, who is willing to work patiently at building its confidence—a difficult personality to deal with.

Independent dogs do not respond well to people—hardly a good bet as a companion. Neither are those that consistently show variable responses to the tests; they have wide temperament fluctuations and are likely to be unpredictable.

For most people, the middle-of-the-road puppy, as indicated by a preponderance of Es and Gs, is the best choice. It is agreeably submissive, accepts human leadership, is readily trainable, and adapts well. It wants to be with people, is affectionate, and has a happy yet sensible approach to life.

On the basis of the foregoing, the following list of traits may help you make your choice.

PUPPY EVALUATION

DESIRABLE TRAITS	UNDESIRABLE TRAITS
Sound	Unsound
Responsive	Fearful
Curious	Aggressive
Interested	Independent
Accepting	Unresponsive
Watchful	Inconsistent
Forgiving	
Dependent	
Willing	

Appendix 3

The Companion Dog's Basic Vocabulary

This is an alphabetical list of the commands, correctives, and words of praise, and their synonyms used in training (see Chapters 6, 7, and 8). As in the text, the basic commands below are set in SMALL CAPITAL letters.

Ah-ah—Stop doing something; mild corrective ("No").
Awright—All right. Sound is drawn out; praise.
BACK—Don't go; command.
C'mon—Come along with, or be in the general area of, the person, to check in if running free; casual, inviting; command.
COME—Immediate response, directly to the person and close enough to be reached; authoritative; command.
DEN—Go to the crate or sleeping quarters; command ("Bed," "Crate," "Kennel").
DOWN—A position in which the body is in contact with the floor, either with the head up and alert (resting position) or flat on one side (sleeping position); command to assume that position.

THE COMPANION DOG'S BASIC VOCABULARY

Drop it—Release something you do not wish the dog to have; strong corrective.

Easy—Calm down; don't be rough; command or corrective.

FETCH—Get something thrown and bring it back; command ("Get it," "Take it").

GIVE—Release a toy or retrieved object; command used in play.

Good boy/good girl—Sound of *good* is drawn out; praise and encouragement.

Go pee—Attend to excretion promptly; command, urgent tone ("Hurry," "Be good").

HEEL—The position in which the dog is on the person's left side with its front legs in line with the person's legs; command to assume and maintain that position, especially in motion.

JUMP—Go over a barrier, into a car, or onto a table; command ("Over," "Hup," "Up").

Let's go—Invitation to go for a walk; a command for controlled walking ("Nicely") or release word for leaving the car ("Okay").

Lookit that pup/Lookit m'boy/Lookit m'girl—Praise and encouragement.

Name—The dog's own name; alerts for subsequent commands, for casual summoning, for conversation with the dog; not a command.

Nicely—Controlled walking, the dog within one to two feet of the person without pulling; command ("Let's go").

No—Stop doing something immediately; strong corrective.

OFF—Don't get up, get off, or don't jump up; authoritative command.

Okay—No longer under control, training is over, or permission to leave the car; release word.

Out?—Want to or need to go outdoors? question.

QUIET—Stop barking; authoritative command.

SIT—A position in which the hind legs are folded, the rump is on the floor, and the front legs are vertical; command to assume that position.

SPEAK—Bark; command.

APPENDIX 3

STAND—A position in which all four legs are directly under the dog; command to assume that position.

STAY—Don't move; authoritative command.

Stop it—Stop doing something immediately; strong corrective ("No").

That's it/That's m'boy/That's m'girl—Praise and encouragement.

WATCH—Pay attention; the dog looks at the person, waiting for further instructions; command (" 'Tention").

Whee—Sound is drawn out; praise.

Whistle—Whistling two or three notes or using a mechanical whistle to summon a free-running dog; command.

You want it?—Invitation to play or retrieve.

You want to go out?—Question used in housetraining.

Selected References

American Kennel Club. *The Complete Dog Book.* New York: Howell Book House, 1985.
Bartlett, Melissa. "A Novice Looks at Puppy Aptitude Testing." *Pure-Bred Dogs/American Kennel Gazette* (March 1979): 31–42.
Benjamin, Carol Lea. *Dog Problems.* New York: Doubleday & Co., 1981.
———. *Mother Knows Best: The Natural Way to Train Your Dog.* New York: Howell Book House, 1985.
Bueler, Lois E. *Wild Dogs of the World.* New York: Stein and Day, 1973.
Campbell, William E. *Behavior Problems in Dogs.* Santa Barbara, Calif.: American Veterinary Publications, 1975.
Collins, Donald R. *Collins Guide to Dog Nutrition.* New York: Howell Book House, 1984.
Cusack, Odean, and Smith, Elaine. *Pets and the Elderly.* Binghamton, N.Y.: Haworth Press, 1984.
Evans, Howard E. "Reproduction and Prenatal Development." In Evans, Howard E., and Christensen, George C. *Miller's Anatomy of the Dog.* Philadelphia: W. B. Saunders Co., 1979: Chap. 2.
Fox, Michael W. *Between Animal and Man.* New York: Coward, McCann & Geoghegan, 1976.
———. *The Dog: Its Domestication and Behavior.* New York: Garland STPM Press, 1978.
———. *The Soul of the Wolf,* Boston: Little, Brown, 1980.
———. *Understanding Your Dog.* New York: Bantam Books, 1977.

SELECTED REFERENCES

Haggerty, Arthur J., and Benjamin, Carol Lea. *Dog Tricks: Teaching Your Dog to Be Useful, Fun and Entertaining*. New York: Dolphin Books, 1978.

Hass, Hans. *The Human Animal: The Mystery of Man's Behavior*. New York: Dell Publishing, 1972.

Kronfeld, David. "Commercial Dog Foods." *Pure-Bred Dogs/American Kennel Gazette*. (March 1982): 8–9.

———. "Dog Foods in the Market." *Pure-Bred Dogs/American Kennel Gazette* (February 1982): 10–11.

———. "National Standards and Generic Dog Foods." *Pure-Bred Dogs/American Kennel Gazette* (April 1984): 8–9.

Levinson, Boris M. *Pets and Human Development*. Springfield, Ill.: Charles C. Thomas, Publisher, 1972.

Mech, L. David. *The Wolf: The Ecology and Behavior of an Endangered Species*. Minneapolis: University of Minnesota Press, 1970.

Meistrell, Lois. "Al and Mona" (an account of testing and training a dog to work with a deaf master). *Progress*, Quarterly Newsletter, Gaines Dog Research Center (Spring 1982).

Monks of New Skete. *How to Be Your Dog's Best Friend*. Boston: Little, Brown, 1978.

Morris, Desmond. *The Naked Ape*. New York: Dell Publishing, 1984.

Pearsall, Margaret E. *The Pearsall Guide to Successful Dog Training*. New York: Howell Book House, 1974.

Pfaffenberger, Clarence. *The New Knowledge of Dog Behavior*. New York: Howell Book House, 1974.

Tortora, Daniel F. *The Right Dog for You*. New York: Simon & Schuster, 1980.

Whitney, Leon F. *Dog Psychology: The Basis of Dog Training*. New York: Howell Book House, 1976.

These two magazines offer up-to-date articles on all phases of dog care:

Pure-Bred Dogs/
American Kennel Gazette
51 Madison Avenue
New York, NY 10010

Dog World
300 West Adams Street
Chicago, IL 60606

Breed books and magazines are available for the most popular breeds. Consult a breeder for references to them.

Acknowledgments

I am indebted to a number of people for their help. Some are close friends of many years' standing who believed in me and this venture; others were discovered in connection with this book. I am grateful to all who gave so generously of their time, advice, editing, photography, encouragement, and support: Judith Haines, Rosalie Siegel, Rhonda L. Hodges Cline, William Mackensen, Jean L. Turner, Mike Johnson, Bill and Peg Johnson, Carol Swart, Marjorie Stewart, Richard and Tirrell Kimball, Gloria Chamard, Kate Moon, Betty Levin, Barbara Kemp, Hal Lauritzen, Nancy P. Johnston, Marlin and Carol Perkins, Richard Wolters, Canine Companions for Independence, and the editors at E. P. Dutton.

Special thanks are also due those patient canines who agreeably put up with the picture-taking: my own Shelties Elspeth, Krysten, and Caitlyn, who are the subjects in most of the pictures; their relatives Rolf, Katie, and Rocky; friends Misty, Ricky, and Bo; and all the others whom I do not even know.

Index

Page numbers in **boldface** refer to illustrations; entries in SMALL CAPITAL letters refer to basic commands. Alternate commands are enclosed in quotation marks.

Age to leave litter, 9–10
Aggression
   disciplinary measures for, 91
   in human society, 40–41
   result of fear combined with, 72–73
"Ah-ah," 58, 72, 74–75, 86
American Association of Feed Control Officials, nutritional standards established by, 131
American Kennel Club, purebred dogs recognized by, 1
Anemia, diet and, 132
Animal shelters, as source for dogs, 8
Anus, inspection of, 148
Appearance, as consideration in choice of dog, 5
Artificial flavorings in commercial feeds, 129
Association, learning by, 67
Auditory sensitivity, evaluation of, 189–90

BACK, 93, 94, 118, **119**
Backsliding, 69, 76–77, 85
Barking, 30, 93–94
Bartlett, Melissa, 186
"Be good," 84
Beating of dog, 78
"Bed," 82

Beds, **140,** 141
Bird dogs, 173, **174**
Biting, 91
   disciplinary measures for, 61
Body language, 37–39, 77
   commands and, 56
   dog's-eye view of, **42–43**
Body openings, grooming and care of, 148
Body temperature of puppies, 14
Bonding, 53–65, **57,** 137
   in humans, 154–55
Boredom, 137
Bowing, as invitation to play, 50
Brain, during neonatal period, 14
Breeders, as source for purebreds, 7
Breeding and selection of dogs, 172–78, **174, 175**
Buckle collars, 102
By-products in commercial feeds, 129

Calcium in diet, 128, 132
Campbell, William E., 186
Canids, dogs' descent from mix of, 167
Carbohydrates in diet, 128
Care and facilities, 127–52
Cars
   etiquette in, 94–95, **95**
   summer confinement in, 143

INDEX

Casual litters, as source for puppies, 8
Character traits of puppies, evaluation of, 195–97
Chewing, 16, 18, 26, 61
Children, dogs and, 165
Chloride in diet, 128
Choice of dog, 1–10
Classes, obedience, 125–26, **125**
Claws, clipping of, 146–47, **147**
Cleanliness, 81, 84
   in yards, 140
"C'mon," 106, 107, 110, 118
Coat, brushing of, **144, 145,** 146
Collars, 97, 100–102, **101,** 103
   position of, **101**
Coloring, 31
COME
   evaluation of responsiveness to command, 191–92
   off-lead, 110–11
   SIT command following, 109–10
   training to, 106–11, **108**
Commands
   aspects of, 54–56
   glossary of, 198–200
   physicality and, 68
   See also specific commands
Commercial dog food, 129–31
Communication, 28–43
   human to dog, 54–65
   mixed signals in, 63–64
Companionship, 158–59
Companionship training
   basic obedience, 96–126
   in cars, 94–95
   housetraining, 79–94
Concentration, learning and, 69
Consistency in training, 83
Controlled walking, training for, 98–102
Conversation, with dog, 54
Copying, 47–48
Correction, 58–62
   praise and, 68–69
Coyotes, 167
"Crate," 82
Crates, **23,** 80, 82, **140**
   in cars, 94
   maximum time in, 83
Crawling, during neonatal period, 13
Cruelty
   respect and, 71
   during training, 78–79
Cuddling, **57,** 84
Curiosity, 20

Dangle of lead, 97, **98**
Death of dog, 179
DEN, 82, 87
Dens, use in housetraining of, 80
Dependence, evaluation of, 192
Development, 11–27
Diet, *see* Feeding; Nutritional requirements
Digging, 90
Discipline
   tactics to instill, 58–62, **59–61**
   whining as appeasement during, 29
   wolves' administration of, 170
Discomfort sensitivity, evaluation of, 191
Diseases, 149–50
Distractions during training, 72, 75–76
Dogs, origin of, 166–67
Domestication of dogs, historical, 173–76
Dominance
   evaluation of degree of, 193–94, **193**
   among humans, 39–40
   among puppies, 50–51, **51**
   among wolves, 168
DOWN, 87, 88, 113–16, **114, 115**
"Drop it," 90, 91

Ears, expression conveyed by, 32
"Easy," 120
Elevators, 92
Embryo, 181–83
Estrus period, 180
Excrement
   earth scratching and, 33
   sniffing of, 34
Excretion, training for, 81–85
Exercise, 134–37, 143
Exploration, 86–87
Eyes, importance in human communication of, 39

Facial expressions, 31–32, 38–39
Family meals, dogs and, 87–88
Fat in diet, 128
Fear, 20–23
   responses during training to, 72–73
Feeding
   myths about, 133–34
   during owner's absence, 83
   of puppies, 82
   schedule for, 133
   in summer, 143
   See also Nutritional requirements
Feet, care of, 146–47

INDEX

Fences, 138
FETCH, 119–22, **121**
Fetus, 183–84
Fleas, 150–51
Fulfillment between dogs and humans, 153–65
Furniture, 84, 88–90

Gender, as consideration in choice of dog, 2–4
Gestures, 38
"Get down," 88
"Get it," 120
GIVE, teaching of, 120
"Go pee," 84
"Go to bed," 87
Gratification, solicitation and, 46–47
Greetings, 44–46, **45**
Grooming
  by owners, 143–48, **144, 145, 147**
  social, 46–47, **48**
Growling, 30, 91
Guide dogs, 163

Hair brushing, **144, 145,** 146
Hair length, 4–5
Handicapped people, service dogs for, 161–65, **162, 164**
Harshness during training, 78–79
Health, as consideration in choice of dog, 6
Heartworms, 152
HEEL, in obedience training, 103–104, **103**
Herding dogs, **175,** 176
Hierarchy within litter, 24–25
Hospitals, role of dogs in, 161
House
  alone in, 92–93
  exploration of, 86–87
Housebreaking, unpleasant association of term, 80
Housetraining, 79–94
  misuse of COME command during, 106
Howling, 30
Humans
  communication among, 35–41
  dogs and treatment of medical problems of, 160
  dogs' relationship to, 157–65
  living world's relationship to, 156
Hunting by wolves, 172
"Hup," 123

"Hurry," 84
Hypothermia, 142

Impositional training, 78–79
Indifference, respect and, 71
Indoor facilities, 141
Inducive training, 28, 79–95
Inoculations, 73, 149–50
Insight learning, 67–68
Instincts, as inherited reflexes, 29
Institutions, animals as part of therapeutic programs in, 159–60
Irish Wolfhounds, height of, 2

Jackals, 167
JUMP, training to, 122–24, **123**
Jumping, 91
Juvenile period, 25–27, **26**

"Kennel," 82
Kibble, 130

Language, in human communication, 36
Lap, puppy on, 84
Laughter, 37
Lead
  COME command training using, 107–110, **108**
  COME command without use of, 110–11
  as communicator, 62, **63, 103**
  exercise and, 135
  not used in JUMP training, 122, **123,** 124
  training for, 97–104
Leadership, in human society, 40
Learning, 66–77
Leg-lifting, territory marking and, 33
"Let's go," 95
Lethargy, diet and, 132
Licking, 90

Maternal behavior, **13**
Meat in diet, 133
Medicine, preventive, 148–52
Meistrell, Lois, 186
Minerals in diet, 128, 132
  oversupplementation of, 134
Mother dog, teaching by, 51–52
Motion sickness, 94–95
Mouth, care of, 148
Mouthing, 90
Movement, retrieval and relationship to, 120

207

INDEX

Name, type and teaching of, 74
National Research Council, nutritional standards established by, 131–32
Neonatal period, 12–15, **13**
Nervous system
  during neonatal period, 12–15
  during transitional period, 16–17
Neutering, 4
Nibbling, 86
"Nicely," 100, 102
Nipping, 102
"No," 58, 72, 76, 86, 89, 90, 91, 94, 102, 104
  need for puppies to learn, 74–75
Noise, dogs' sensitivity to, 73
Nonvocal communication
  among dogs, 31
  among humans, 37–39
Nutritional requirements
  basic, 127–31
  feeding myths and, 133–34
  individual variations in, 131–33
Nuzzling, 46

Obedience classes, 125–26, **125**
OFF, 87, 88, 89, **89**, 90, 91
"Okay," 95, 100, 102, 118
"Out," 81, 82
Outdoor facilities, 138–40, **138, 139**
  free running in, 90
"Over," 123
Overprinting, territoriality and, 33
Overstimulation of puppies, 24
Ovum, 181

Parasites, 150–52
Pawing, 46
Paying attention, 75–76
Pen, for puppy, 141, **141**
People, respect for, 88–91
Personality, molding of, 6
Pet quality, definition of, 7–8
Pet stores, as source for puppies, 8–9
Phosphorus in diet, 128, 132
Physical corrections, 61
Pinning tactics, as disciplinary measures, 59–61, **60**
Plants in yards, 139
Play, 48–50, **49, 50**
  exercise and, 136–37
Posture, dominance and submission and, **51**
Potassium in diet, 128
Pounds, as source for dogs, 8

Praise, 56, **57**
  correction and, 68–69
Prenatal development, 181–84
Preventive medicine, 148–52
Problem solving, dogs' ability to learn, 67–68
Property, respect for, 88–91
Protein
  in commercial feeds, 129, 130
  in diet, 128, 132
  oversupplementation of, 134
Punishment, discipline compared with, 58
Puppy evaluation, 185–97
Purebreds, 1–2, 7

QUIET, 93–94

Rabies, 150
Repetition, learning by, 67
Reproduction, 180
Retrievers, **175**, 176
Retrieving
  evaluation of ability of, 194–95
  training for, 119–22, **121**
Rooting reflex, 12
Rugs, 84
Running, 134–35

Scenthounds, 173, **174**
Self-control, during training, 64–65
Senses, information received from, 67
Service dogs, **162, 164**
  for handicapped people, 161–63
  insight learning by, 68
Sexual maturity, 27
Shaking, as disciplinary measure, 58–59, **60**, 87
Shedding, 5, 146
Show dogs, 177
Sighthounds, 173, **174**
Signal dogs, **162**, 163
SIT, 94, 104–106, **105**
  COME command prior to, 109–10
  STAY command with, **113, 116**
  training to, 104–106, **105**
Size, as consideration in choice of dog, 2
Skin problems, diet and, 132
Sleep, during transitional period, 17
Slip collars, 100–102, **101**, 103
Smacking, as disciplinary measure, 87
Smell, communication and, 32–34
Snarling, 91

208

INDEX

Sniffing
　acceptability of, 86
　of excrement, 34
　as social greeting, 44–45, **45**
Social behavior, 44–52, **45, 48, 49, 50, 51**
Social needs of humans, 154–55
Socialization period, 17–25, **18, 19, 21, 22**
Sodium in diet, 128
Solicitation, 46–47
Sound, puppies' reaction to, 15–16
Soundness, as aspect of health, 6
SPEAK, 94
Specialized types of dogs, 173, **174–75,** 176
Spinal cord, during neonatal period, 14
Stairs, 92
STAND, training to, 117–18, **117**
STAY, 87, 94, 111, **111,** 112
　DOWN command with, **115**
　SIT command with, **113, 116**
　STAND command with, 118
　training to, 111–13
"Stop it," 58, 90
Strangers, 73–74
Stress factors, diet and, 132
Structure, evaluation of, 186–88, **187**
Suckling reflex, 12
Supervision
　freedom and, 136
　of puppies, 82

Table manners, 87–88
Tail, mood denoted by carriage of, 31
"Take it," 120
Teething, 18, 26
Temperament
　companionship and, 158
　as consideration in choice of dog, 5–6
　flexibility of, 70–71
"'Tention," 76
Terriers, **175,** 176
Territoriality
　urine scent and, 33
　among wolves, 168–70
Tethers, 135
Ticks, 151
Timing
　while disciplining, 58
　while praising, 56
Togetherness, 54, **55**
Toilet, outdoors, 81

Touch
　dogs and human sense of, 160–61
　evaluation of sensitivity to, 188–89
Touching of puppies by strangers, 73
Toys, 92–93, 136
Training
　BACK, 118, **119**
　collar, 97, **101**
　COME, 106–11, **108**
　companionship, see Companionship training, consistency in, 83
　DOWN command, 113–16, **114, 115**
　exercise and, 136
　FETCH, 119–22, **121**
　HEEL, 103–104, **103**
　JUMP, 122–24, **123**
　with lead, 97–104, **98, 99**
　of older dogs, 124–25
　process of, 68–70
　self-control during, 64–65
　SIT, 104–106, **105, 113,** 116
　STAND, 117–18, **117**
　STAY, 111–13, **111, 113,** 116
Transitional period in puppy development, 15–17, **16**
Trial-and-error learning, 67

"Up," 123
Urban pressures, 155–56
Urine, scent as communication, 33
Utilitarian roles for dogs, 176

Vaccinations, 73, 149–50
Vision, 35
Visual sensitivity, evaluation of, 190
Vitamins in diet, 128, 132
Vocal communication
　among dogs, 29–31
　among humans, 36–37
Voice, feelings conveyed by tone of, 36–37
Vomiting reflex, 46

Walking, training for lead-controlled, 98–102, **99**
WATCH, **75,** 76, 102
Water in diet, 128
Weakness, diet and, 132
Weaning, 19–20
Weather, 142–43
Wolves, **169**
　coloring of, 31
　discipline among, 170
　encounters between, 170–72

INDEX

Wolves *(continued)*
    facial expression of, 32, **169**
    group organization of, 167–68
    howling by, 30
    hunting behavior of, 172
    knowledge of canine communication derived from, 29
    nuzzling behavior in, 46
    sniffing behavior in, 44–45
    territoriality among, 168–70
Worms, 151

Yards, 135, 138–40, **138–39**
Yelling, 69
Yelping, 30
"You want it?," 119
"You want to go out?," 81, 82